Dirty Breath: Trapped by Rejection

A Memoir

Lana M. Hooks

This book is dedicated to God for teaching and showing me that He is not what I learned from the man's learned slave teachings, bondage, insecurities, and low self-esteem. The freedom He gives in mind, body and soul requires a price and that is death to belief systems that are born out of rejection, and its many evil constituents that we accept and believe out of ignorance. Ignorant derives from the Greek word "agnoeo." It means *without knowledge or understanding of.* [1] Knowing and understanding the foundation of the belief system empowers you to disembowel the dysfunctional mindset to transform your thoughts and your life to authentically live emotionally healthy.

My life experiences are examples for you to better understand how to glean from your own lives the wisdom that was brought to you in adversarial times. I utilize medical and spiritual terminology that pertains to **my** journey. It is only to be used as a guide for you to research what may be your "dirty breath." If you are presently taking medication or in counseling this memoir does not suggest or prescribe any change to your regiment. It is an account of the steps that I had to take on my journey. Please continue to seek Godly wisdom and counsel if what you are currently doing is of great help to you.

I have also changed names or not used a name at all to protect the identities of the innocent and the guilty. More importantly, I want the genetic code, emotions, and behavior birthed of my experiences to be emphasized more so than the name of the person.

Permissions Acknowledgements appear on page 246.

Published by PharSide Coed Book Club, Inc.
Printed by CreateSpace

Front & Back Cover Design: Ariana Rivera
ariana@arianarivera.com
Author's photograph: P&P Photographer
Brandonperry92@hotmail.com

PharSide Coed Book Club
ISBN: 978-0-9835797-0-0
ISBN-10: 0983579709
www.pharsidecoedbookclub.com
Printed in the United States of America

Emotional abuse of a child is commonly defined as a pattern of behavior by parents or caregivers that can seriously interfere with a child's cognitive, emotional, psychological or social development. Emotional abuse of a child — also referred to as psychological maltreatment — can include: Ignoring, Rejecting, Exploiting or Corrupting, Verbally Assaulting, Terrorizing, and Neglecting the child.

http://www.americanhumane.org/children/stop-child-abuse/fact-sheets/emotional-abuse.html

It is an honor and a privilege to be a steward of a child. You have the greatest charge in unfolding and viewing a portion of the gifting and talents that the Creator planted of Himself in His greatest creation – huemanity, a child. Don't ever take it lightly when a child is on your watch. You have a front row seat in viewing God manifest Himself and share Himself with you. LMH

PharSide Coed Book Club

Many roots, many voices are a part of the Infinite story...
Plant your seed...

CONTENTS

CHAPTERS

Foreword

What Emotional Legacy Do You Want to Leave Your Children?

Genesis 35:11: "And God said unto him, I am God Almighty: be fruitful and multiply; a nation and a company of nations shall be of thee, and kings shall come out of thy loins."

Our children are the fruit of our loins. Fruit: Latin word *fructus* meaning enjoyment, profit. Loin: Latin word *lumb* meaning by extension, the lower back which supports the whole body structure.

If, in fact, our children are the fruit of our loins, then it would seem befitting for us to treat them as the kings and queens they are from the thought of inception. As Ms. Hooks has so eloquently written, from the time she was conceived, the words of her grandfather to her father with her mother being present *"Well, you got what you wanted, she's pregnant now, and you've soiled her for all other men. No one else will ever want her."* When these words were uttered, and heard by Ms. Hooks in her small fetal state, it created an everlasting impression on her memory cells, her soul and her thoughts. **The brain remembers every sound, every**

7

feeling, and every thought even though the rest of the body is not yet formed.

If we want to serve ourselves and humanity justly, then we will prepare our children in this life for the many challenges they are sure to face. They will be better equipped, more confident to face these challenges head on. You will see a child full of certainty, strength of character and a determination to succeed. This book will help you to begin that journey.

Sandy Beauford Muhammad

Member of The Nation of Islam

Apology

To **All the People** past, and present that I've mistreated, hurt, disappointed, or abused by thought, word or deed, and wounded in soul **I SINCERELY APOLOGIZE** for my actions towards you. I was emotionally not in the present and my soul was asleep due to childhood traumatic events. I was operating out of the entities *Rejection, Fear, and Mis-Trust*. No, this is not an excuse, but this book is an explanation, all twenty-nine short chapters of it. From the womb to Fifth grade I breathed in familial generations of the entities *Rejection, Hurt, Shame, Pain, Fear* and *Self-hatred*. I learned unhealthy ways of how to protect myself because no one else either knew how or would protect me. I didn't know how to respond to people from an authentic and emotionally healthy mindset. All I knew was I wished I was someone else because being the authentic me didn't seem to be good enough.

The aftermath of failed relationships and not being emotionally present in them led me on an inward journey to understand who I was at the age of twenty-eight. As I did the mental, emotional, spiritual and physical legwork of facing painful memories, my question, challenge and purpose became, "If I had children what emotional legacy did I want to leave them?" Did I want to leave them the emotional, behavioral tsunamis caused by *Rejection, Abandonment, Fear, Perfection,* of *Hurt* souls in my family? No, I want them to know they can honestly express their thoughts and behavior without fear of verbal or physical backlash. I want to teach them of course balance and self-control, but in a nurturing environment to protect their esteem and affirm their self–worth. My goal is to ensure their emotions are kept authentic and healthy so their behavior, personality and character are not compromised to act, think, and exist with a *Hurt* person's belief system thereby operating in a schizophrenic mindset. This is the premise of my memoir, what I fought through and my purpose in life.

Parents leave their children monies, land, businesses, and other material wares, but do they think to pass on to their children authentic emotional health? Authentic emotional health is being allowed to be emotionally honest. By definition emotional honesty, according to Steve Hein, "Emotional honesty means expressing your true feelings. To be emotionally honest, we must first be emotionally aware. This emotional awareness is related to our emotional intelligence. It is our emotional intelligence, combined with the necessary learning, practice and experience, which gives us the ability to accurately identify our feelings."

There is a freedom in operating in one's authentic emotions, which in turns produces healthy behavior and esteem. To authentically identify our feelings, and function out of self-love where one's unique personality has been nurtured in an emotionally safe environment will instill and build non-judgement, kindness, compassion, gratitude, healthy relationships, peace, self-respect, joy, and love. No one can put a price on these invaluable traits.

As you will read, damaged, poisonous emotions were passed down to me from past generations. These learned behaviors affected my ability to identify my authentic emotions. It also skewed my definition, perception and interpretation of female and male relationships, definition of family and authority figures, work ethic, and character traits of God. From the spiritual advice I sought counseling at the age of twenty-eight to figure out at first what was wrong with me. Why didn't my family like me? Why was I fat? Why couldn't I have a boyfriend? Why didn't cute boys like me? Why was I either needy, enabler, or nurturer in relationships with females? Why was I the "other" woman who chose to be in non-committal relationships with men? Why did I allow close people to verbally and sometimes physically hit me? Why was I so afraid to speak up and defend myself? Why I became sullen and silent when things didn't go my way? Why did I walk away from relationships? Why was I afraid of confrontations? Why did I not want children or to be married? There were so many why's that I needed to find out what was wrong with me first and then later in life find the real me, the authentic me. I lived under the muck and mire of *Hurt* soul's words that metamorphosed into a belief system in which I believed I wasn't good enough to be the real me, whoever that person was.

I went back to where it began - my childhood. Beginning in the womb of my *Hurt and Rejected* mother and sealed at the age of ten. I physically carried *Rejection and Hurt* as fat (*Obesity* [I hate that word]) on my body by ingesting and believing every insulting word a *Hurt* person infected me with. Those early events as you will read manifested as sickness and dis-ease in my late thirties and forties. I was diagnosed as Pre-Diabetic, Cervical Disc Degeneration, and Sciatica. I learned later, closer to my fifties, that being fat and rejected was my protection, but that is a whole other beast and another book. But I knew it was imperative in counseling that I find out what was wrong with me, and who was the culprit that stole my original identity, my emotions and behavior, and lastly, my physical body.

It was an urgent call in me to allow myself to "re-member" (find the buried pieces in my soul) my authentic emotions. I wanted to identify and freely voice my authentic thoughts, behavior, and words. I wanted to see me, the person created by the Infinite God. But first I had to confront all the other *Hurt* souls I allowed to live inside my soul that was wreaking havoc in my body. This is that journey back to the womb of my mother until the age of ten, where I was trapped and raped by the entity *Rejection* and later on its family members.

I truly hope and pray that by the end of the last chapter you understand, while not justifiable, why I responded unseemly in relationships that went awry. And again, I humbly ask for your forgiveness. Thank you.

Sincerely,
Lana M. Hooks

Gratitude

To the people who took their time to get to know me and saw my insecurities, low self-esteem, mood swings, ugly ways and silent, sullen moments but loved me and stayed around me anyway – THANK YOU!!!

You looked inside of me and saw what God wanted you to see (so you could tell me) even when I vigilantly believed the lies of my past. I am forever grateful for those at Indiana University (The Rainbow Coalition), and Bethel A. M. E. Church in Bloomington, Indiana. Also to the wonderful and supportive people I met at Indiana State Fire Marshall's Office, and deceased president of Martin University, Father Boniface Hardin, who gave me a second chance to earn my undergraduate degree. I had two wonderful friends that worked for the postal service in Indianapolis, Indiana. They left me the most inspirational cards in my mailbox. Those cards made me believe that someone could like me? The wild and loving ladies and guys I met at Martin University y'all were and still are the bomb. Lastly, those creative, wild, funny and loving folk I met in Atlanta who befriended me when I wasn't looking for a friend but God told you otherwise.

Thank you for not physically hitting me or verbally bashing me even when we were joking around or you correcting me. You loved me in spite of myself and for those precious moments of knowing you I am forever changed.

I purposely did not give names because of obvious reasons, but I know you know who you are.

Teaching me how to Love,
Lana

WE WEAR THE MASK

We wear the mask that grins and lies,
It hides our cheeks and shades our eyes, - -
This debt we pay to human guile;
With torn and bleeding hearts we smile,
And mouth with myriad subtleties.

Why should the world be over-wise,
In counting all our tears and sighs?
Nay, let them only see us, while
We wear the mask.

We smile, but, oh great Christ, our cries
To thee from tortured souls arise.
We sing, but oh the clay is vile
Beneath our feet, and long the mile:
But let the world dream otherwise,
We wear the mask!

Paul Laurence Dunbar

Introduction

It is my desire to not see another child or adult move through life trapped in *Rejection's* intricate web. Judgmental attitudes, being held hostage verbally/mentally/physically by generational, cultural, and religious beliefs which also attracts (and you accept) unhealthy relationships. These ultimately hinder growth in being your authentic self.

It is only through Divine intervention one seeks to "know thyself." Emotional abuse is damaging not only to your behavior, but also physically to your body. My aim is to guide you in understanding how abused emotions directly affect your behavior and body.

Your abuser was abused. It's a vicious cycle that fortunately can end, but you must be willing to undergo the task. These learned behaviors can be unlearned through identifying your authentic emotions. *Awareness* and *Forgiveness* are major allies in releasing those *Hurt* souls that verbally, physically, or religiously bashed your emotions. *Forgiveness* is your release into behaving with your authentic emotions and living your life in freedom.

You are uniquely created huemans born with a specific genetic code in your DNA. In each family there are emotions and behavioral patterns that reveal themselves in physical and verbal or non-verbal cues. You must pay strict attention to those destructive patterns and behaviors that you witnessed and experienced first-hand in your biological families. As you grow up the scope of your environment

16

lengthens to include other systems like religious, social, or educational organizations. Those patterns you first encounter in your families will more than likely be subjected to in the aforementioned systems.

The highest form of living is to think, act, and speak as a genuine, authentic being without extreme *Rejection, Fear,* and *Shame* controlling your behavior. To not behave as an authentic being is called 'emotional dishonesty.' Constantly berating a person's thought, not allowing them to voice their thoughts, and utilizing physical punishment as a tool of control will force that person's soul (mind, body, and emotions) to go to sleep. That place is called *Unawareness* and eventually *Non-Identity*. The child (that will grow up to be an adult wounded child) consistently subjected to abusive treatment learns to mask their authentic behavior; thereby, living and breathing someone else's energy in thought, word, behavior and will eventually manifest in the body if the Divine does not intervene to make them *Aware* of what is occurring.

This is what happened to not only my mother, but I believe in generations prior to my initiation into the spirit of *Rejection*. I breathed in her *Rejection* while in her womb. Our relationship was the catalyst for this memoir. I believe if she had a healthy emotional foundation, felt protected, and loved, in which all huemans deserve, she would have publicly been the greatest griot, teacher, writer and poet of her lifetime. Her voice, her story, our relationship sets the tone and heart for this memoir.

Purged

I had always been their friend, their pal, and their running buddy. They would always come and talk to me about their problems. I could play with them. I liked stickball, tag and kick the can. I was the chubby little girl, the buddy, the play interest, and the good ole pal.

Growing up to pre-teen that was fine. Then pre-teen is over and you've begun to be interested in boys because you are of the opposite sex. They are not interested in you because they still see you as a buddy and not as a girlfriend. Growing up that was fine!! Then you begin to see guys as a love interest, or puppy love, you know that teenage angst that most of us go through? You get older and the angst turns into the real thing about one guy, but he is thinking of you as the stickball player. That is when it begins to hurt.

That's when if your love is not returned, you turn. If you have no one to direct you, you turn and go in the wrong direction. You are no longer the chubby little girl, you are the fat teenager and everyone else is pairing off into couples but you're left alone. Still the stickball player and the shoulder to cry on by the guys about their girls (always the bridesmaid, never the bride). None of the guys looking at you with hearts in their eyes for you.

Then comes along the smooth talker, an older man, you think that you are in love. He says all of the right things, pushes all of the right buttons. You are ripe for any and everything. You think that you are in love. But all that you are ripe and ready for is the fall, this great, big, hard fall. It sounds so good, but it is all talk. No one in your peer group has ever talked to you like this before, but for one reason and that was a buddy. You are so naïve, you fall for it hook, line and sinker.

It takes little persuasion, but you give him your most precious gift, the one thing that you should have held on to until the right man came along. But you are starved for love, no, not love just male attention that you give it up for trifles, for nothing. This was your virginity! Immediately you want it back, but it's too late. Once it *is given it cannot be retrieved. You both are careful. You are not out of high school yet and you do not want a baby. That's because everybody thinks that is what is going to happen anyway. They keep saying, "She's too quiet, I know she's messing around with someone. Still water runs deep." Up until then when you met the older man it had all been in your head, because no one else wanted the little fat girl. Things go well for a few months, but this is a sneaky, forbidden romance because he is a full grown man and you are just a little girl a little fifteen year old girl, an immature fifteen year old at that. A baby, a child, that's all you are, but have the body of a woman. Who would not believe that you did not seduce this man? You read a lot, you know about sex. But you only know that sex is from a book. No one has explained what can happen in reality. No one has sat you down and lovingly told you why you should wait, why you should not do this, why you should do that. You've gotten it in bits and pieces from your mother, from the school nurse, from friends in the bathroom, and from him. He is setting you up for what he wants from you. You are sooooo naïve.*

Finally, in 1961 you graduate from high school. You have been blessed, you have not become pregnant. Shortly after graduation things get hairy. You get lazy and careless. The funny thing is you are pregnant and don't even know it.

One day you hear your father talking to whom you thought was your secret lover, but all the while your parents know what you have been doing. You thought that you had been so careful. Your folks didn't know. I have since learned upon becoming a parent myself that parents are very astute. But I overheard my Dad say to him, "Well, you got what you wanted, she's pregnant now, and you've soiled her for all other men. No one else will ever want her."

Hearing this from your Daddy's mouth you are cut to the quick. It hurts so much your heart is broken. You feel little and deep down you know that no other men will ever want you. Your own father said you are soiled. You know what soiled means. It means dirty.

Daddy said it so it must be true. This colors the rest of your life. You know that no other man will want you, you are degraded.

A few weeks later when go to the doctor and find out for yourself that you are really pregnant, you tell him officially and that's when things go awry. He swears to you that the bay is not his and that he will pay men who hang out on the corner at Twenty-fifth to say that they all had you and that I don't know who the baby's father is. This is when I see him for what he really is. On top of all this he begins to go out with a lot of your so-called friends and acquaintances behind your back.

After you catch him and whom you think was your best friend sneaking out of his apartment you try to kill them, but by the grace of God, you don't know where your mother got the strength to hold you off of them. You don't know, but it had to be God because you are larger than your mother. But she somehow holds you back because you had a straight shot at stabbing the girl to death and then you want to go after him next. You are eight months pregnant and your mom tells you that she cannot raise another child so you cannot go to jail and have my child in jail.

Shortly after this incident, he comes to you and says we can get married, but when we do you can only do as I say. He wants you to separate from your family, friends, and everything that you know and hold dear. Death had already separated my father and me. He had died a few months after making the statement about the soiled daughter. He tells you that if you talk to your mother on the phone he must be on the extension. If you visit your mother, he must be there with you when you are speaking with her at all times.

That is when you discover that he didn't mind hitting a woman. That is when you discover that you cannot marry this less than nothing. You begin to wonder, what did you see in this person? You learn that you did not like this male let alone love him.

The relationship with him gets worse. You stop seeing him as a boyfriend and lover. This relationship plus an incident that had happened to you when you are truly a child, only seven years old, colored even more all of your relationships with all men. This was something you try hard never to remember but sometimes it surfaces.

When you are seven a family friend touches you in inappropriate places for a grown man to touch a little girl. He has you touch him also. Then he tells you that, "this is our little secret. You can't tell anyone, not your mother, not your father, no one for this is our little secret." You hate that sentence until today. It denotes dirty and nasty things, slime and filth. At seven you don't know. You don't know any better. You don't know it is wrong. He tells you, "it was all right and that it feels good." How are you to know, you are just a little girl, a baby, only seven. Years later, after he is dead, you remember you can't tell anyone. You are still scared.

These two episodes in my life marred all of my relationships with all men. They made me turn to the wrong types of men. All of my friends were falling in love and getting married, and I was just having babies. I love them all, I love them then and I love them now. But just for once I wanted a man to fall in love with me and want to marry me because he is so in love with me that it hurts. Back then I wanted the same thing and to have a child in love and not just sex. I wanted to marry him and he would love my other children and treat them as his own. Now that they are all adults and it's just me, I would like for him to come to me just because he loved me. Automatically he will love my young adults.

Now in my more mature years I am learning that I am not soiled. I am God's child and am worthy of a God fearing good Christian man's love and affection. Now that I'm past childbearing years, and that's okay by me, I have four wonderful adult offspring some married and some not, but all self-sufficient.

21

At this stage I'm still asking the Lord to send someone who will love me and spend the rest of his life with me. But I am learning that it is all right if it's just me and my wealthy old Jewish man who is preparing a heavenly home for me. We'll just court each other and I'll be satisfied.

I CHOSE "PURGED" FOR THE TITLE BECAUSE NOW THAT IT IS DOWN ON PAPER, I HOPE IT IS OUT OF MY SYSTEM AND CANNOT CONTINUE TO HURT ME AS IT HAS DONE FOR SO LONG.
Annie K. Boyde
(Hannah Grace)

It took my mother fifty-one years to speak of this horrid event. She was an innocent seven year old trusting a "friend of the family." She didn't remember if her parents knew about this "friend of the family's" perverted act. If they did, they never addressed it. The times dictated this as an unspoken subject, a secret, a taboo to not talk about. You didn't dare air your family secrets. If I had not been compiling an anthology in 2001 of people who had overcome or was in the process of overcoming insurmountable odds I don't think she would have told me. She left it on my bed to read and when I finished unanswered questions from years past and unfinished counseling sessions resurfaced in me. Questions about why my weight was viciously attacked by family at more times than I care to remember? Why she didn't defend me when other family members bellowed at me, or called me out of my name, or publicly shamed me? Why did she leave me with my younger siblings for days to fend for ourselves? As I stated earlier, I had questions about my childlike, distant, or silent behavior as an adult. Why did female/male relationships go awry? I was confused about my sexuality, unrecognizable and fear of my voice, of people, amongst

22

other things. Needless to say her story unearthed my past with a vengeance. But first, to explain my mother's silent behavior regarding the sexual abuse the answer did not come until ten years later.

In 2011, one day a friend of mine texted me about a cause he's passionate about GM (Genital Mutilation). Female Genital Cutting or Female Genital Mutilation is a horrible procedure done to women in Northeast Africa, Near East and Southeast Asia. It is, *defined by the World Health Organisation as "all procedures that involve partial or total removal of the external female genitalia, or other injury to the female genital organs for non-medical reasons (http://en. Wikipedia. org/wiki/Female_genital_cutting).* But that night as I thought of the subject the Divine spoke to me after a dream and said that is what happened to me and the women in my family, only he added the word "emotionally" before the words "genitally mutilated." Allow me to share the dream and explain the origin and meaning of this procedure.

One early morning I dreamed I was in the church I grew up in Gary, Indiana. I do not have many fond memories growing up there because of the slave teaching's on sex and hellfire and brimstone, and some of the adults' and my peers' treatment towards me. These influences were a major contribution to the squashing of my authentic self. *In this dream I laid down on an offering table that was in the front of the sanctuary. It looked more so to me like a doctor's examining table. I opened my legs and a woman put a steel clip on my clitoris and it was chained to a small steel ball. I remember getting up off the table and feeling the ball touched my anus. I was aroused as I walked out of the church and into the street.* I woke up shocked, and while lying in bed, I asked God what just happened.

The term Emotional Genital Mutilation came to me. Genital Mutilation is generational, and also a religious and cultural

23

tradition. This procedure is performed on a young girl so she will not be a social outcast and for lesser reasons to preserve her virginity, and dull her sexual enjoyment. Societies who practice this feel this is necessary to properly raise a girl to prepare her for adulthood and marriage. The medical issues that arise from this procedure are urinary tract infections, obstruction of urine and menstrual flow, scarring and infections among other sicknesses. This is not to mention the emotional and mental scarring of a young lady.

Talking with the Spirit about the term EGM (Emotional Genital Mutilation) the Spirit applied FGM (Female Genital Mutilation) as a backdrop and partial definition for EGM.
I don't remember any biblical teachings that were taught in an emotionally, healthy and balanced way, especially when it came to sex. As an adult when I did have sex I saw my grandmother on one shoulder telling me *you know this is wrong* and on the other shoulder a voice said *you are going to get pregnant like your mother*. Needless to say I've never "injoyed" intimacy. I was never emotionally present and I always felt ashamed of my body. So my enjoyment became, well, you will read later what it became. But just like most women who were taught under strict religious teachings they were Emotionally Genitally Mutilated. They wore; I wore a steel ball and chain clipped to our/my clitoris that rubbed our/my anus. Remember in the dream the steel ball touched my anus and I was aroused. According to the online <u>Dream Moods Dictionary A-Z</u> "anus" means, *"To see your anus in your dream signifies negative emotions that you may be holding in and repressing. It represents feelings of guilt, shame, and self-worth..."* *(http://www.dreammoods. com/dreamdictionary/a3.htm)*

This is why my mother couldn't tell her parents about the sexual abuse that was done to her. She was *Ashamed* and

24

blamed herself for that horrible act. She thought she initiated that "friend of the family" to inappropriately touch her and she him. She repressed her authentic emotional honesty and lived thinking she was not worth it to tell her family. She was Emotionally Genitally Mutilated as women in my family before her and particularly of that era. Partially it was the religious teachings taught (and believed) in an unhealthy or an ignorant manner that stunted me and my mother's creativity, and the physical, mental, and social growth process as you will read.

This memoir is not about revealing my family laundry for the sake of it, but recognizing from my early years emotions and behavioral patterns that deterred me from being my authentic self. Even though I am writing this from a female perspective, it is not just for females but males as well. In an unhealthy emotional female dominated household, males are affected as females. *Hurt* single females will see their son as a reflection of how they "feel" about his father, or their father. She will either use him as a "little husband," to fulfill the duties of a father who is not present in the home, or, she will emasculate him, or, prayerfully not, sexually abuse him, fulfilling her inordinate desires.

Rejection is my family's curse and gatekeeper coupled with its nasty offspring as you shall read. I knew I had to confront it head on. For as long as I can remember I was emphatically told by family, so-called friends or those who chose to agree silently that something was wrong with my behavior, my body, and my creative brain. Consistently with these *Hurt* souls towards me that stated I was "wrong," I interpreted that to mean "I am wrong." I am wrong for being chubby, for the way I think, the way I write, and the way I talked and walked. In essence, I was the embodiment of "wrong." My emotions, thoughts, and my behavior became so skewed and misunderstood that I began to live anyone else's reality, and speaking and thinking their

25

language. I wore the mask of those around me in church or school that my family showed a fondness toward. It got to the point that everywhere I went I stole the identities of anyone that I or my family was partial to because I already knew beforehand no one was going to like me. After a while I didn't know where "I" was and quite frankly I didn't care. As long as people didn't abuse me in any manner, I remained the clone of the "liked" person as I witnessed my mother in her circle of acquaintances.

I realized my mother's story and my family's curse is not exclusive. Other families have experienced far worse than we did. I also write this memoir for those families that have children or planning to have children. I realize there are no instructions or books that give you a precise and detailed overview of how to raise a child. But if you are willing to open your eyes, stand flat footed and honestly look at your family tree, you will see how, what, and who you want your children around to raise them in (as much as you can) a healthy emotional environment.

The early violation of my mother's innocence tail-spun into events that shaped her emotions, thoughts (belief system), that later manifested into sickness and dis-ease in her body. From a little girl and that perverted conduct from a close, personal, family friend, a teenager and my father, to an adult, jaded her thoughts of the one institution a child is supposed to feel safe in - family. There is an old adage that states, "We can't choose our families, but we can choose our friends." What happens when **you** don't choose people to be your "friend"? Also, what happens when the institution called family, especially at an early age, fails to choose to protect, lives in fear, or, forgotten how to protect you? Unless there is strong Divine intervention, all other relationships, institutions, i.e., religious, educational, law enforcement, etc., will not be trusted as well.

I pray this opens up dialogue and you will explore your family tree to seek out your emotional authenticity and go heads up with what's trapping them and you into a false reality. I realize not every family will be saved from horrific circumstances and it will be necessary and appropriate for a specific purpose that you must go through them. But if my story can assist you in explaining the birth of powerful, destructive and corrupting behaviors, then this book was worth the emotional, behavioral and physical battles I've endured and prevailed thus far.

I also write this book for my father who passed away in 2010 before it was published. He was a result of his past as well. And even though he was not physically present in my house, it did not exempt me from his emotional and dysfunctional behavioral patterns. He too lived in a house called *Rejection* and his treatment of me defined my relationships with men and God.

I do believe if he had an emotionally solid foundation as well, on how to be a man and father, he would have been physically and emotionally present in his children's lives. Also, if given the chance he would have been a great historian. Little did I know when I asked him if he had the chance to attend college, what would he have studied? He said, "History. I've always loved history." What was my major in undergraduate and graduate degrees? It was African American History. His answer explained my fascination and love of not just information, but peering into the lives and behaviors of people from different cultures.

Finally, I write this book to complete an assignment by my God. As He told me of late, "You are not responsible for the outcome; your only responsibility is to be obedient. The rest is on Me!"

In Forgiveness, Self-Acceptance & Learning How to Love,
Lana M. Hooks

RE-MEMBER

1

Scars of Rejection

In late 2001, sitting at my desk with my headset on waiting for a call (but hoping one didn't come in) and reading an inspirational book I saw my beginning from a nonphysical vantage point.

I love to read about people's spiritual/supernatural experiences. It amazes me to see how God, Creator, Holy Spirit, Truth, the All Knowing, Consciousness, whatever name you are acclimated to interact with mankind. As a side note, I will interchangeably use other names God is known by as well. God is a Spirit not a gender (I will refer to the Trinity in male terms). Also, God has given me the freedom and the ability to discern other spiritual and/or secular works outside of Christian theology that explain the character, biblical text and beliefs of the Trinity as well.

This freedom, in the Spirit, has enriched my relationship and understanding of the Trinity. It has endeared me to love the ways in which the Divine interacts with huemanity. It has broadened my learned myopic view of the Divine and to dispel an ignorant belief system as well. When you search for Truth, keep your eyes open, it can come in varied forms and trust me, you'll not lose sight of who you serve. It's His

Love for you and your search of Truth that will keep your focus clear. Now back at my desk...

This man's father died when he was an infant. The Holy Spirit asked him, now married and with his own family, did he miss his father. He thought it a strange question to be asked since his father died when he was an infant. Exploring the question more the Holy Spirit stated everyone born is innately given to know the touch of their biological parents. And if infants aren't consistently touched by their parents, they will know by either having a strong desire to seek and find their parents, overcompensate in childhood and act like a parent themselves, or become a mentor in adulthood.

This man knew only his mother's touch, but as an adult, he mentored young men and spoke on the importance of father's being in their children's lives. In spite of his mentoring programs and teachings on fatherhood the Holy Spirit told him he didn't have a chance to grieve his father's death. The man, prompted again by the Holy Spirit, allowed his feelings, his thoughts, and the unspoken words in his heart to surface to grieve the father he never knew, a father who never touched him.

Needless to say reading his experience was blowing my mind. I was trying to wrap my mind around how an infant, a baby knows the missing presence of a biological parent versus an adoptive parent, or a divorced parent who remarried? But then I saw images of adults on talk shows that were adopted as infants wanting to find their birth parents. Even though their adoptive parents/step parent loved them, they still felt as if they were missing something or didn't belong, especially if there were birth children in the family. My question was answered while another one entered my mind. A call comes in.

Thank you for calling in. May I have your name and address please?

"Are you going to ask me the question in your mind?"

Truth would speak to me now when a call comes in.

Thank you for your information, Ms. Smith. Just for security reasons may I have the last four digits of your social security number?

"I really don't know if I want to know the answer."

Thank you Ms. Smith. Now, how may I help you?

"Ask the question."

Okay, the room you want the extra line in is it on an interior or exterior wall? I understand, let me explain what both are. If the wall you want the outlet on has a window and you can see outdoors then that is an exterior wall. The interior wall means there is a room on the other side of it. Yes, I will hold while you check.

"It feels like a dumb question, or totally out there, and I …"

"It's not a dumb question. Just ask it." Truth is unrelenting for me to ask the question in my mind.

"Okay, I know my birth mother and father's touch, but their presence was inconsistent and rare in my early years. Nevertheless, I do know their touch. The constant presence and touch was my Mama's (grandmother) from outside the womb and early years. But I still felt abandoned and alone. I really don't know my parents (at this time my parents were still alive). So my question is what happened in the womb of my mother?"

You know in the movies when someone is having a flashback the room spins around, well, in my case it didn't. But my eyes were wide open, the noise in the room minimizes and I am propelled back to my mother's womb. I realize I am experiencing an open or waking vision.

I am a fetus. Actually, I'm in a dual role like a person who is dying and floating above the scene, seeing everyone around them. That is what I'm experiencing. I can see her cells, veins, arteries, heart and the umbilical cord connecting me to her. I hear men talking.

"Well, you got what you wanted, she's pregnant now, you've soiled her for all other men. No one else will ever want her."

Those words knocked the wind out of my mother. One hand is holding her stomach and the other over her mouth. She wants to run. But that will reveal her hiding place from her father and my father. I look up at her throat. Something phenomenal is happening. The words, she heard her father say to my father are being swallowed down her throat. You know, like on Sesame Street where each letter is alive, with its own energy and has a personality of its own. She's not breathing. I'm choking. The letters/words are moving faster down her esophagus. I looked over at my mother's heart, it's beating exceptionally fast. I hear a voice say "heart attack." I see the letters from the words of *Dirty* and *Soiled* clogging up her organs and arteries. There is a slight tear in her veins. They are very thin and are erratically moving. I hear a voice say "butterfly veins". The words are almost near my living quarters. I can't move. I want to escape, but I'm trapped in her womb. My mother is crying and silently repeating the word *Dirty*. She knew that was what *Soiled* meant and it was trailing right behind *Dirty*. With each repeated word I'm being saturated by them like an oil spill on a baby duck. They are sticking to me, embedding into my embryonic state. These words are now united with my mother's established tainted belief system (*Hurt, Rejection, Low Self-Esteem* and *Pain* of her early childhood molestation and teen

33

rejection of no boy her age asking her out). This is not only how she feels about herself in her soul, but the words' energy by definition have become a part of her musculoskeletal system, her skin. And since the umbilical cord connects us I now believe what she believes because her father, a significant authority figure spoke, gave life and energy to those words. She and I are *dirty* and *soiled*.

Ma'am, are you there? Ma'am? Did she leave me?

I hear Ms. Smith calling me, but I'm feeling disconnected, faint even. I manage to respond.

No, ma'am. I'm here. I was just making sure we have earlier dates for your order. I'm sorry I didn't answer you when you first called me.
Well, I just didn't want you to leave me. I know I took a while, but I do want the outlet on the inside wall.
Okay, well give me a moment. I'm going to add everything up, but first let me go over your entire order so I won't miss anything and then I will give you your total.

I go over her order and she is satisfied. I asked to place her on hold, she permits it. I begin to fill in her order. My fingers are moving across the keyboard. I don't feel them. Another vision comes into view. This time I hear my father and mother talking.

I am pregnant. I went to the doctor today and he confirmed it.

My father is mad.

I am going to pay the men who hang out on Two-five to say that they all went to bed with you and that I don't know who the baby's father is.

It is at this moment I scream! I mean I see and hear me screaming as a fetus. I fling off my headset. I didn't want Ms. Smith to hear the scream in my head. I still see me screaming in her womb. I am screaming, *why doesn't he want me?! Why doesn't anybody want me?!* The vision is gone.

My head was filled with air. My legs were released to run to the bathroom. I needed a drink, yes, and a good stiff one at that. I'm sorry I left Ms. Smith hanging on the telephone line, but I've never had an open vision that was so vivid. Even my dreams weren't that graphic or detailed. I then understood how a need can be unmet, even in the womb. The old adage *you can't miss what you've never had* is a lie from the pit of hell.

A scripture I'd read became alive in that moment of revelation. *Death and life are in the power of the tongue, and they who indulge in it shall eat the fruit of it [for death or life]* (Proverbs 18:21, Amplified Bible). Spoken words released from living, breathing vessels carry energy of life or death. At that moment I breathed in generations of negative energy *(Rejection, Abandonment, Betrayal, Fear, Pain and Hurt)* of my paternal and maternal family. I was not born in a welcomed womb, but a wounded womb.

These visions showed me how *Hurt* [to feel or suffer bodily or mental pain or distress] people, *Hurt* people. When my mother swallowed her father's words (*dirty, soiled*) she stopped breathing and I was choking as a fetus. When my father told her his plans to pay other men to say they slept with her, these words added to her *Hurt* (from her father and "friend" at seven years old). Everything she felt, I felt. I screamed. Everything she believed, I believed, and as I grew up those words and more spoken to me affected and formed my mind (thoughts, belief system), body (sickness and disease) and soul (formed wounds) as did she and those before her.

The belief systems deeply rooted in the *Rejection* of my paternal and maternal lineage were so extreme that it manifested physically on my body as keloids, systolic cyst and acne, stunted height and obesity. Did I have a chance to make it out of her womb unscarred? Indulge me for a moment to give you a natural and spiritual backdrop of these physical conditions. This won't take long, I promise you.

The medical definition of a keloid is, *Keloids are raised, reddish nodules that develop at the site of an injury. After a wound has occurred to the skin both skin cells and connective tissue cells (fibroblasts) begin multiplying to repair the damage. A scar is made up of 'connective tissue', gristle-like fibers deposited in the skin by the fibroblasts to hold the wound closed. With keloids, the fibroblasts continue to multiply even after the wound is filled in. Thus keloids project above the surface of the skin and form large mounds of scar tissue* http://www.aocd.org/skin/dermatologic_diseases/keloids_and_hypert.html).

A cyst is a closed sac-like structure that is not a normal part of the tissue where it is found. Cysts are common and can occur anywhere in the body in people of any age. Cysts usually contain a gaseous, liquid, or semisolid substance. Cysts vary in size; they may be detectable only under a microscope or they can grow so large that they displace normal organs and tissues. The outer wall of a cyst is called the capsule. Cysts can arise through a variety of processes in the body, including:

- *"wear and tear" or simple obstructions to the flow of fluid,*
- *infections,*
- *tumors,*
- *chronic inflammatory conditions,*
- *genetic (inherited) conditions, and*

36

- *defects in developing organs in the embryo* [bold italics, mine] *(http://www. medicinenet. com/cysts/article. htm#tocb)*

Isn't it amazing that with keloids the tissue continues to multiply over the same wound even after it's been healed? It seems the wound doesn't know it has been healed and continues to transmit to the tissue to keep repairing the damage. HM... Cysts can arise from defects in developing organs in the embryo (the words of my grandfather and father rejecting my mother and me, saturating her heart and mine as a fetus). The plot thickens, continue to read on. It's almost over.

A friend from Zimbabwe bought me a book for my birthday in 2002, *A More Excellent Way, I Corinthians 12:31 – A Teaching on the Spiritual Roots of Disease by the Ministry of Pastor Henry Wright.* Before he was called to the ministry, he was studying to be a doctor. His medical preparation gave him the knowledge and credibility to speak in this area which greatly benefits those in the medical and spiritual profession. When I read the spiritual diagnosis of my inherited conditions, I threw the book across the room.

The spiritual root of cysts, according to Pastor Wright is *the breakup of the relationship between the girl and her mother. Unresolved issues involve a great breach, and there is no fellowship. It carries right down into the reproductive area. It involves a full issue of femininity. It is involved, even to the degree that the girl may question her own femininity, or the female part of her creation. The mother has breached it at that level. Many times there is great bitterness, anger and great resentment toward the mother. I have found it true, coast to coast, that the people who have been healed of ovarian cysts, breast cysts, and systolic acne have had to get things right before God concerning their mothers.*

37

He was right. My mother and I had an estranged relationship. I always thought my Mama, my grandmother was my mother. My mother was, to be honest with you, a person that occupied space with me. We both later stated we didn't know each other or ourselves.

This knowledge coupled with Pastor Wright's diagnosis of *Obesity, is fear of man, fear of failure, fear of abandonment, fear of rejection, lack of self-esteem, and introspection where you look inside yourself and you don't like what you see.* I know that book was tired of me throwing it across the room. This pastor had hit both spiritual diagnoses on the nail. Finally, it was making sense about my dysfunctional behavior, the lesions on my body and why I rejected my body.

These natural and spiritual definitions described in great depth how words and unmet needs of *Hurt* people, if believed to the very core of the soul (mind, body, emotions), wound it and can manifest as sickness and dis-ease in the physical body.

As you have seen I italicize and capitalize entities, i.e., *Rejection, Awareness,* etc. Words can hurt or they can heal. In order for them to perform by definition they must attach themselves to living, breathing, energy filled hueman souls. I will also spell "human" as "hueman." We are different ethnicities but share a Spirit connection.

I was a wounded fetus from the wounded womb of my mother and the self- indulgent wounded sperm of my father. After this experience I wasn't shown that no one physically or verbally abusing me. Going into my third year I was introduced to the supernatural and a host of entities that were waiting for me.

My desire and hope for you is that as you continue to read my story, pictures, snapshots and fragments, of your past will resurface so you can see the entities (negative energies) and the masks (false identities) they brought that you've worn for years. And when you are *Aware* and recognize them, I pray that you allow the Holy Spirit to unearth your authentic emotions and behavior so you can finally live your purposed life and breathe *your* fresh air.

2

In The Beginning: Truth

My Mama (grandmother; I will refer to her as Mama) in whom I ate, bathed and slept with was there before and during my birth in nineteen sixty-two until her transition in nineteen seventy-seven. She was **my** mother, my rock, and protector of my life. From a baby until about five or six years of age, she was a part-time maid working for rich Jewish families who seemed to treat her exceptionally well. They gave her clothes, shoes and handbags that came from prestigious and select stores and boutiques. When my Mama was at work sometimes I stayed with another family. They had two daughters, I adored. It was fun being treated with love and kindness as if I was their biological little sister.

Periodically, though, I would go to work with Mama and play with the grandkids of a Jewish family. Early on I was aware of skin color from a declaration I made to my mother. I told her that I was White (as if it was more beautiful than her color) like the Jewish family, which also included my babysitter and her two daughters (they were very fair skin but still Black) and I impudently told my mother she was Black (as if it was something dirty). I didn't even know how I knew the term black and what it meant. It just came out of my mouth. My mother quickly set me straight on the racial terminology of White and the different shades of Black or back then Colored but my mother preferred the term Black.

She didn't participate in the Civil Rights Movement. She later told me that Mama was afraid she would be killed and didn't want to take care of me as an older, mature adult. In order to fulfill that desire my mother's participation was reading Black history books to newspapers, both, Black and local newspapers of the events that were occurring in the south and north. Needless to say after that discussion color was not an issue. I played with the Jewish children knowing my ethnicity and it didn't change my relationship with them at all.

On the weekends my mother came home to Gary, Indiana from Chicago, Illinois. During the week she lived with her oldest brother and his wife working at the infamous Hilton hotel as a switchboard operator. But the majority of the time I was with my strong, Christian, protective Mama.

My mother and I on occasion did spend time together. I remember one story that my mother told with such awe, fear and love. I realized later in life that as she told this story, it was her way of letting me know that she was in my life while her own guilt was assuaged. But each time she told it unanswered questions lingered in my mind long after the last word was spoken. This story was my first memory and indoctrination into the realm of the spiritual/supernatural followed by many unexplained visions and dreams.

I am around two almost three years old and I am playing near the rocking chair. My mother is in the kitchen preparing dinner. She hears me talking and asks me who I am talking to. I tell her Granddaddy.
Now my grandfather died six months before I was born, so I should not have had a clue of what he looked like.
She told me that my grandfather was dead, and I politely told her, "No, I am talking to him." I also tell her, "I passed him as I

was coming in." I described in detail his blue/gray eyes, spit can, and satin shirt. My mother runs out the back door and leaves me sitting on my grandfather's lap. My Mama returns from work at dusk to find her daughter sitting on the steps with no grandchild beside her. She explains to her mother what happened earlier. They both are scared to come into the house, but eventually they do and find me asleep on the floor.

The funny thing is I do remember this occurrence, but not all of what he said to me. And I didn't know what it meant, and why me? What I do know is that moment with him, at two and a half years of age, in the dining room something sinister took place. The *enemy, devil, Satan* wanted to kill me because of who I am to God. Truth imparted this knowledge to me as I sought an answer why the visitation. Please stay with me because this does get real spiritual/supernatural, but I will try my best to explain it in practical terms.

Small children tell adults all the time they see things (scary or comforting), hear things or have dreams about people they've never met, but their stories are sometimes discounted. It reminds people of supernatural occurrences they've experienced, were pushed to the side by authority figures in their life, and told to be quiet. It therefore becomes a mute topic and the child is dismissed as the otherworldly encounter.

Visitations of the deceased, as well as dreams and visions must be explored and dissected to know what it means, why this particular child, and what is the will, purpose and destiny of your child. Even if you aren't comfortable or don't know about the spiritual or supernatural realms just ask someone you believe you can trust and go on gut feeling. If you sincerely seek Truth, Truth will present itself in a way that is familiar to you. Let me give you an example of what I mean.

When the first *Harry Potter* book and movie came out, there was great controversy in the Christian community as to why children shouldn't read or watch the movie. The obvious was it contained witchcraft, sorcery, demons and creatures (as does the Bible, go figure). This uproar was for fear that children might be seduced into the occult and open them up to domains that possibly could influence their minds and souls. There is soundness to this belief. Who are we to arrogantly believe that there are not realms beyond this world that want the minds and souls of children? But, as a parent or guardian you must ask and seek Truth to know who your child is and what their purpose is in life. You may be surprised that your child is supposed to watch certain movies with you by their side to answer their questions. Trust me they will have questions and insight. Age has nothing to do with innate wisdom. All I ask is please don't shut down your child's questions or feelings (emotional dishonesty- a youngster not being permitted to convey their true emotions or thoughts) because you may not be capable to explain or are afraid of what you'll learn about not only your child but also yourself. It is okay not to know the answers at that moment. You must trust that you'll be led to the answers.

When the movie came out I didn't speak against it. I remained *Silent* for *Fear* I would be *Rejected* by those same circles. Actually, I didn't watch it until a year later when it was telecasted on the HBO channel. I sat on the couch in my favorite navy blue house gown, with a glass of White Zinfandel, cheddar cubed cheese and crackers excitedly awaiting *Harry Potter and the Sorcerer's Stone.* Two hours and fifty-three minutes later with tears in my eyes, I knew for years to come that I would watch the sequels. What my Mama and mother couldn't and didn't know how to explain to me about dreams, visitations and visions this movie prompted me to begin that journey.

The visitation from my deceased grandfather was explained in several ways. Truth explained in the stories that my mother told me of her father along with information that only Truth would have known. That moment with my grandfather, I couldn't remember all of what he said to me. It was not until I watched this movie that it gave me the courage to seek Truth, ask, and pay attention to how, and what Truth would reveal about his visitation.

My mother's first-hand insight and statement to me was he was lazy, mean, and called her siblings belittling names. Several detrimental things happened to our family as a result of his laziness. He allowed millions of dollars to slip right through his hands. Let me explain. Slavery robbed him of his original family. His biological father was also his slave owner. He was rejected by his father for obvious reasons. Being detached from his ancestry, family origin and father resulted in a young boy who was emotionally detached and mistrusted people outside of his race.

His father's last name was Boyle. When slavery ended, he changed his last name to Boyde. My mother told me how he hated his father as well as the Caucasian race. And as a constant reminder of his birth parent, he was cursed with gray, bluish eyes while his dark skin reminded him of being enslaved. Pieces of the unhealthy emotions and behavior of my grandfather through this knowledge explained his decision in the following narrative.

During WWII a Jewish man he worked with told him that if he went round the city with him picking up wire hangers the government would compensate them for it because they needed it for building war planes. My grandfather told him he was not going to pick up nothin'. His hatred of captivity, the disowning of him by his Caucasian father, resulted in an emotional, psychological damaging effect, thereby his hatred of self and the Caucasian race. He missed a golden opportunity to become wealthy and leave a financial legacy to his family. In contrast the Jewish man became one of the richest property owner's in Gary, Indiana. His children will never have to worry about anything unless they squander it.

Slavery in America was monolithic in and all by itself, leaving a legacy of psychological damage in its wake. My grandfather's soul was deeply affected by being the extremely dark rejected son of a slave owner. The *enemy* used those wounds to transfer to me damaged emotional behaviors in the womb of my mother.

My mother, who was in the kitchen, asked me what he was saying to me. I told her that he said, "I passed him on my way in." But what bothered me for years was what ELSE did he tell me? Truth won't divulge that information to me. Maybe I don't need to know. But what I do know is as I grew up I acted out the emotional legacy passed to him of his family. It is clear to me what transpired generationally has greatly affected me and my family emotionally, physically, mentally, socially, financially, and spiritually.

These entities (in which I see as life extracting energies) *Rejection, Laziness, Self-Sabotage, Self-Hatred, Self-Rejection, Mean Spirited, and Pride* were an emotional legacy passed to my grandfather, his children and lineage. Even though it didn't start with him, his behavior stayed consistent of his lineage as well.

Right before he died, he was going into his "second childhood," a colloquial term to describe Dementia or first stages of Alzheimer. He heard voices speaking to him and he'd say things at random. A key point to remember from this point on is that **he heard voices**. My mother was three months pregnant, and he told her that he knew "her secret" as she was changing his diaper using a bed sheet. My mother told me she hadn't told anyone about her pregnancy. He mockingly laughed at her which kind of scared her.

There are evil *spirits,* much like *entities* only worse, that attach themselves to wounded souls to make life's challenges feel like you're in the very pit of hell. But Truth will take moments, situations, and horrendous experiences and use them for your good, even though you don't see it while you are in the midst of them. You just have to *Pay Attention*, be *Aware* and usually 20-20 vision comes after those crazy, awful times. But I truly pray you seek Truth coupled with *Courage* (positive life giving energies) to really look at those moments to receive *Clarity*. You are an authentic being, born with a purpose and a destiny, no matter what you've gone through. Know this!!!

Truth also revealed to me the *enemy* told my father to tell my mother to abort me. He thought it best for my mother, but truthfully he didn't want to take care of another child. *Abandonment* was the emotional legacy left by my father's father. As told to me by my father, his father worked on the railroads and was gone most of the time. This left him to drop out of school, take care of his siblings, never marry (as far as I know), never own a house, drive a car or really do the things he wanted to do in life. He didn't know how to be

46

a father because his father did not possess those traits to be an example for him. He was not emotionally or physically consistent in my life as his father did to him. I learned the same behavior by the age of ten. I learned to *Abort* people who *Rejected, Abandoned* or *Hurt* me.

If I had not watched a movie banned by the very community I'm a part of I might not have had the courage to seek Truth and certain things may not have been revealed to me. As I stated before Truth comes in many forms. I was mature enough as I watched the movie in my own spirituality and relationship with Truth to know what applied to me and what didn't. But it's up to parents to be very discerning to eliminate what doesn't need to be revealed too soon or not at all to a fetus or a young mind. Some situations, words and feelings you can't push in a corner and told to be quiet. Your children's lives are depending on you to open up and speak to them about what you do know about your family and what you don't know Truth will reveal at the right time.

I believe that if the traditional religious community knew the freedom of Truth (in the way Truth wants to present it to the individual), and not a doctrine to keep man enslaved to an offering plate, the member's only club, a restrictive and obligatory theology, and the four walls of a building, I sincerely believe spiritually, emotionally, mentally, intellectually, financially and physically it would be a mature body that would operate from a *Higher Consciousness*.

ASSESSMENT: Before this moment I had a great Fear of the unknown, fear of Truth, fear of researching further to see what the dreams/visions meant. I believed in the status quo of religion as the final word while negative entities controlled my soul.

WISDOM: I'm not speaking against any one religion, faith, or belief, but I am speaking out about not listening to your child and hearing what they are really saying. Don't take a religious system's word as the final say in your life. The only one reserved for that position is God. Just sit quietly and ask out loud the help you need. If you have never walked inside a church, it's okay. If you really want Truth you need to ask and Pay Attention to how the answer comes. And be open to see the answer in any form it chooses. More than likely it will come in a form you are comfortable with already. Mine was movies (with and without supernatural content), television (cartoons, Anime) and reading (African American fiction/non-fiction, Self-help, Children's books, & other books on spirituality outside of Christianity, Paranormal, and Speculative Fiction). These are just some of the vehicles that Truth uses to talk to me. He is quite practical and wants to answer your questions just like He did mine.

Look at your family's history and see what is really in the tree, it doesn't take magic to do that. The Harry Potter movies are just vehicles to open up honest, real dialogue regarding entities that attach themselves to wounded souls in unresolved family issues. It only takes a willing heart, a still body and a talk with Truth to hear the cries of things spoken and more than not unspoken. Your child's mental, emotional, physical life, spiritual life and destiny depend on it.

Your Memories of
Pictures, Snapshots, or
Fragments
(Write, Draw, Doodle,
Color, Scribble)

3

Vaseline Black Patent Leather Mary Jane Shoes & the 23rd Psalms

Yellow frilly dress and bobby socks trimmed in white lace and my black *Mary Jane* shoes shining from Blue Seal Vaseline, I was sharp as a tack. My hair is in a small, very small, bun up do. I looked like a princess. I am walking happily between my Mama and my mother's hand in hand to the big church on the corner. They are having a program where I am scheduled to recite the 23rd Psalms from memory. My Mama taught me passages of the Bible before I learned to fully read. In fact, she had me recite chapters from memory, not verses, no that was too easy. I was Miss Annie Mae's granddaughter.

At first I enjoyed memorizing chapters, poetry, speeches it was fun to see the words in my head when I recited them, but shortly, thereafter it became a burden. My Mama stretched me to go beyond people's expectation. I don't know if that was good or bad. The jury is still out on that case.

The auditorium is packed with people. I wasn't nervous just excited. I hear my name called and my mother says, "Do good now." I walked toward the side of the stage where a man is standing to assist me up the stairs. Walking in the middle of the stage I stood confident in my Vaseline Mary Jane shoes. I hear the ooh's and ah's of the people, but I'm looking for the familiar faces of my Mama and mother. I see them and I begin to recite the 23rd Psalms. The room was quiet except for the "look at that baby" comments as I was halfway through the passage. When I reached the ending "and I shall dwell in the house of the Lord forever" the people were standing on their feet. I smiled like the Cheshire Cat in the *Alice in Wonderland* story looking at my Mama and mother. They were pleased. I walked back toward the side of the stage where the same man is waiting to hold my hand to escort me down the stairs. I was greeted at the end of the stairs by my mother. She and I walked back to our seats as people gave her accolades about my recitation.

Yes, I admit I liked the attention, it made me feel great, but I wasn't seeking the attention. This was a pure unadulterated moment. I was just happy to share the moment with Mama and my mother. Little did I know that feeling great would be few and far between. Entering the age of three was off with a blow that left its mark until this present day.

> *MASK/Behaviors: NONE!!!*
> *I had a pure moment with my Mama and mother.*

4

Pierce That Baby's Ears: A Witch's Touch

I'm three years old and visiting my mother, uncle and his wife in Chicago for the weekend. I loved my uncle's wife. She was so beautiful to me. She was short and petite like Dorothy Dandridge and had pecan brown skin like Sarah Vaughn and always dressed in the latest fashions. She was a lady in every sense of the word. Her and my uncle stayed in a very nice brownstone with furniture of the era. If you look at *Mad Men*, a series about the sixties, the furniture of that era is an accurate depiction of how their brownstone was furnished as the clothing. If you haven't seen the shows allow me to give you a brief description. Imagine if you will a six foot wood encased stereo with brass handles, wood liquor cabinet, and white embroidered cloth furniture with heavy wood pedestals or feet and no plastic covering on the furniture. My uncle despised plastic coverings and white stockings. He said if you're not a nurse don't wear them. This was their home.

One night my uncle was having a get together with his friends and my baby uncle was there too. I don't know how the subject came up but the women wanted my ears pierced. The men objected especially my baby uncle. I remember bits and pieces of going to a home that was huge, almost castle like. The couple were Caucasian, but with an accent and wore black clothes. They had a huge fireplace with a straw broom on the side of it. The lady went over to the broom and retrieved two straws. My uncles were pissed because they didn't trust the woman. They thought she was a witch. Her husband wore all-Black and he had an earring in his ear too. He brought out wine. I remember him, saying it was from his country. They drank it, but like an eagle eyeing his prey, my baby uncle never stopped looking at the woman preparing to pierce my ears. Amongst the protest the women said, "She's going to look so cute" or "All cute little girls get their ears pierced." My mother told me later she wished she had spoken up and not gotten my ears pierced (me too) but that is water under the bridge now.

The woman sat me on her knees, told me it wasn't going to hurt, and to be a big girl. I looked into her dark eyes with deep black mascara drawn on her lower and upper eyelids. She wore huge earrings that hung down to her shoulders. By the time I realized any pain the needle with the straw pierced my ears. It was over, a done deal. My baby uncle, like an eagle to its young, swept me up in his arms and we left.

Once back in Gary my ears were doing fine. My mother kept them clean and I only wore pure gold earrings. But one day she felt a small bump in both ears. She and Mama did double duty in cleaning them, the right one went away but the left kept growing. My baby uncle found out about the bump in my ear and he swore the woman who pierced them put a curse on me. I've often wondered why my ears were touched and left scarred. Researching "earlobes" from the **Dream Dictionary** means, *alternatively, it means that you want to stand out and be different. You want to go against the norm (http://dreammoods.com/cgibin/dreamdictionarysearch. pl?method=exact&header=dreamsymbol&search=ears).* Other spiritual references ears to the prophets and hearing words. This woman's touch to my ears possibly was another piece of the *Enemy's* plot for me to hear and believe verbal abusive words. Any positive words I heard were met with unbelief.

A few years later I was referred by my Jewish doctor to a Black colleague, the best in the city. We went to Dr. Gregory and he informed my mother that I had keloid skin. I had to stop wearing earrings. Did this mean I wasn't cute anymore? In my mind it did. Were my ears touched by a witch? Don't know, but my uncle was a believer. I wasn't a cute little girl anymore because I was touched and "possibly" cursed by a witch on a cold night in Chicago.

MASK/Behaviors: Self-Image   questioned,   Low   Self-Esteem, Unknown hands touching my ears

UNMASK: My mother confessed to me when I was older that she blamed herself for allowing people she knew and didn't know to hold me as a baby and a little girl. People were drawn to me and wanted to hold me and kiss me. She thought they were nice and meant no harm. She learned later in church about the motives of the heart and word curses people can speak over you. This knowledge made her wonder was the woman really a witch who pierced my ears.

Those who have children, with child, desiring a child or caregivers don't let everyone touch your children. I know it's sad to say, but not everyone you know may like you and they may have ill will in their hearts. And because of the trusting nature of some children they are easy prey for retaliation. If you are pregnant, don't let everyone touch your stomach. My friend wore a shirt with a nice saying on it to ask her permission to touch her stomach. I admired her courage, forthrightness, self-respect and respect for her child. Her love for her unborn child on her shirt spoke great volumes to me. Don't allow everyone to touch your child.

"Only those with pure hands and hearts, who do not practice dishonesty and lying," Psalms 24:4 (The Living Bible).

Your Memories of
Pictures, Snapshots, or
Fragments
(Write, Draw, Doodle,
Color, Scribble)

5

Bicycle, Bicycle, Bicycle, Bike

My first birthday party was in 1967 and I was turning five years old. It was filled with people dancing, playing games, eating and music. My three favorite friends were there Sandra Rae, Diane and Darryl (*all names have been changed*). We all lived on the same block. Other friends of the family were there, including my babysitter and her daughters celebrating with me. In a couple of months I would have another surprise too.

My father didn't come to the party, but there was a present, a two-wheel bike. I don't remember if he or my mother gave me this gift. But this was his MO with me, (he left the gift or the money asked for but his presence was pretty much ghost) until I was a young adult and I chose to get to know him.

Sandra Rae, Diane and Darryl knew how to ride a two-wheel without the training wheels. They all agreed they would teach me how to ride without mine too. Diane was two-years older than Sandra Rae, Darryl and me, but it didn't matter, we were all good friends who played and had great fun together.

When summer came the neighborhood was alive with activity. Kids were out playing, the cow and pig were being sacrificed on the pit and Martha Reeves & the Vandellas were, "Dancing in the Streets." Sandra Rae, Diane and Darryl were riding their bikes and I wanted to ride mine. My mother brought my bike outside and told me how far I could ride mine down the street, which was down to Darryl's house and back. I rode my bike proudly with my training wheels intact. It was my first time and I had to get used to it. We rode and raced each other daily until one day I was told it was time to learn without the training wheels. Admittedly, I was scared but my friends were there to help me learn.

My mother took the wheels off and I got on with her on one side and Diane on the other holding the handlebars. I started peddling with them, guiding and holding the bars and establishing my balance. They gradually let go and I did okay, but then I lost control. I tried to take control and steer, but *Fear* sets in. I needed my mother and Diane to hold the handle bars. I felt protected, but without them, I felt alone and scared. I was *Embarrassed*, but Darryl helped me back up and I tried again. This went on for a while, but I just couldn't maintain my balance on my own.

Finally, my other relative who was sitting on the steps said, "You can't ride a bike because you are too fat." This was the first time I remember those words said to me. My chest became hot and I felt *Ashamed* of my body. Here I was embarrassed in front of my friends, and *Hurt*, especially by a close relative in whom I thought loved me. Those words also gave license to Diane to use against me. Sandra Rae and Darryl felt bad for me. I could see it in their faces. I didn't want them to look at me like that. I got back on the bike and tried again and again and again, until finally I gave up. My relative's statement had deeply offended and wounded my soul. The spirit of *Offense* found the open wound (*Rejection*) made in my soul in my mother's womb. *Offense* ignited a *Fear* in me toward significant people in my family by those who *Abandoned* or let go of me. At that moment I agreed with my family's unhealthy belief system about weight and size; and, being fat I couldn't ride a bike (and to this day I still can't). I only rode it (with training wheels) when Sandra Rae and Darryl were around. Diane eventually stopped playing with us. Darryl gave it one last try to help me, but by that time I believed in my soul that being fat meant I couldn't learn to ride a bike. Darryl strongly desired for me to learn how to ride a bike, but when I didn't, all I saw was pity on his face. That was the last look I saw on his face. He moved away from the neighborhood shortly thereafter.

Even though I greatly feared of trying new things in later years, what I feared more so was the people and their taunting words about my weight. Certain people in my family, some members of the church I belonged to, and select teachers in school held my emotions and body hostage in telling me I was fat. When I heard those words my mind froze as my body because I was fixated on what they spoke to me. I *Sabotaged* my ability to perform in the activity. Also the pattern of *Divide and Conquer* was set with my three friends by my relative. I wasn't good enough to be their friend. I was flawed because of my size. This belief system followed me into every relationship I've ever had. As I grew up that relative who told me I couldn't ride a bike, I felt, got a personal kick or some sort of revenge for embarrassing me in front of friends and peers. When she screamed at me or berated me in front of peers this also gave them license to say I was fat too. But later I learned from Truth she did it to hide her emotional wounds, I was the scapegoat. I also learned her *Hurt* was far greater than mine.

My self-image was built on other *Hurt* soul's that learned an unhealthy perception of their self-image. I have lived my life operating in someone else's unhealthy feelings, thoughts and belief system. Therefore I used my weight to dictate my participation in life. It formed and shaped my viewpoint in

58

a female to female relationship and female to male relationships. The few sincere female friendships I had, I always thought I was the flawed one in our relationship. I also put them on a pedestal refusing to see their insecurities or flaws. My distorted perception of me skewed my view of people in general. I only saw myself as the matronly, fat, battered victim. I feared masculine men who had not been touched by another man because I was fat and not good enough to be with them. I was deathly afraid of guys who may have liked me because of self-hatred. I wouldn't have noticed if they did. I take that back. With the exception of two men in my life who told me and kindly showed me, but outside of those men I couldn't differentiate if any other man may have sincerely liked me or me imagining that they did. Lastly, relationships showed me how body differences were rated. And being fat was at the bottom of the chain.

鼓 *MASK/Behaviors: Fear of being Abandoned, Fear of being Embarrassed, Hurt, Spirit of Offense, Ashamed, Fear of family, Fear of female and male relationships, Victim, Sabotage, Divide and Conquer, Comparison, Competition, Low Self-Esteem, Self-Rejection, Skewed Self-Image, and not good enough to be a friend*

UNMASK: Children don't know what they look like until they are told by a significant person in their life. I didn't know I was fat, and the truth of the matter I was chubby. I began to look at females and compare their bodies to mine. If they were bigger than me, I felt better about myself, but if they were smaller than me or a little chubby I would find some body part I liked about them and covet it. If they were petite I wished with everything in my heart to look like them.

I guess talking about my weight was my relative's use of reverse psychology to get me mad enough to lose weight. But obviously it didn't work. I just knew each time I felt brave to try an activity I felt being fat I couldn't do it. Be it an activity where I used my mind or any talent I had. I felt embarrassed or ashamed just because I was fat. I was flawed and not good enough. And this was the process each time - I was embarrassed or ashamed. My chest felt like it would cave in. My face and body became extremely hot and my legs went numb. I could hear the air fill my head and it felt like it wanted to explode. Fear immobilized my mind and body pushing me to sabotage my effort. I honestly believe if those words had not been spoken to me, I eventually would've learned to ride a bike later than my friends did, but no matter, I would have learned.

Please understand all children learn at different rates and their body structure doesn't determine if they can or can't learn an activity. It is the love, patience, encouraging words, healthy discipline and paying attention to your child's way of learning that will determine the rate in which they will grasp what they like or dislike. Choose words that help instead of wound the soul.

> Your Memories of
> Pictures, Snapshots, or
> Fragments
> (Write, Draw, Doodle,
> Color, Scribble)

*To my sister Kimberley I wouldn't trade anything for you. I truly hope you forgive me for this ugly moment in my beginnings. I am so glad that the Lord put you in my life. It is not my intent to hurt you by adding this horrid moment in my memoir. But it is to explain how far, even at an early age, a *Rejected* soul can think or do unspeakable acts. Kimberley I truly hope you forgive me as I've had to from time to time forgive myself. I love you!*

6

I Don't Like Surprises

For five years I was the only child and I liked that arrangement. I didn't have to share with anyone unless I wanted to. I honestly don't remember anyone telling me about this surprise that came a few months after my birthday party. I just remember looking at the bed and there she was, my sister. She was pretty. Her skin was the color of a *Reese Cup* and her hair was thick, dark and curly. It surrounded her head like lamb's wool. But I didn't care if she was pretty. I didn't want her living in my home. I knew that she was a baby and she couldn't take care of herself, but I wasn't prepared to share my space, place, and the attention of my family. Yes, you are correct I was *Jealous* of this pretty chocolate baby that everyone ogled over as if I didn't matter anymore. I was deathly afraid that those who still loved me (my Mama) would stop and leave me because she was the prettiest chocolate baby with all that hair.

My babysitter came to our house one day and I was so happy to see her. Of course, I knew she was coming to see me, she was on my side, I thought. She came in and acknowledged my presence and asked where the baby was.

In my stomach I felt a sharp pain. This woman who knew me from an infant wanted to see the new baby. I felt betrayed, but I didn't give up that easy. Each time I got a chance to squeeze in getting some attention I did, but it didn't work. She looked at my mother and said, "Someone is *Jealous* because they are not getting attention." She tried to convince me that a baby needed more attention than I did and I was growing up. I wasn't a baby anymore. They laughed at my futile attempts for attention. I walked away and started playing with my toys. I stayed to myself the entire time she was there and when she said goodbye *Hurt* responded to her. I was five years old, *Jealous* and *Envious* of the new surprise. Oh, but *Jealousy* took me to a whole new level that sometimes even now I'm still repenting for my actions.

A few months later I was taking a bath, enjoying the bubbles in the water, basically having fun by myself. My mother entered the bathroom with my sister in tow. She told me to hold her while she went to get something, I can't remember what it was. I protested loudly. I mean I was angry at my mother for bringing my sister in on my time. She looked at me and said I better hold her and not let go of her either. I held my sister under her arms. My mother left the bathroom. The more I looked at my sister the more *Jealous* I became. Since she had grown her skin was rich and earthy. Her hair was fuller and thicker where mine was thin and scarce. Everyone who saw her fell in love with her skin color and hair. I felt like I was nothing now that the real person they wanted was here. I just whet their appetite, the main course had arrived. This feeling of being "never good enough" was growing on me as weight and in me.

I removed my hands from under her arms. She immediately slipped underneath the water. I saw her fighting, but I didn't help her. I wanted her gone from my life, so people who once loved me would love me again. What was I thinking? Sensing danger my mother ran to the bathroom just in time to grab her from under the water. Yelling, screaming, crying and turning my sister over to clear the water from her little body she told me to get out of the tub. I was trying to *Lie* my way out of this situation by telling her she was moving too much and slipped. With a towel wrapped around my body I walked to the bedroom not knowing what to expect. My sister was lying on her stomach crying, but she was fine. Before I knew what hit me my mother had a wet rag in her hand and commenced to beating the living daylights out of me. My towel betrayed me. There were no bounds on my body where that wet rag did not hit. Naked and unashamed has a whole new meaning for me now in light of this vile memory. With each hit she was asking me why I did this and between each huff and puff that if I ever harmed her again she would kill me. I twisted my body better than any contortionist trying to evade the wet rag that had become dry after she finished whipping me. She told me to put my panty's on and get in the bed, turn my face toward the wall and don't get up until she told me too.

When I got older I talked about this with my sister as well as another horrible statement I told her when I was older. I use to tease and tell her she was adopted. And she thought she was because of her skin color compared to the rest of our siblings. I know I was the mean, ugly big sister. You can say it because I said it to myself until I asked her to forgive me, and blessedly she did. But not until I wrote this I realized I hadn't forgiven myself.

I am the oldest child of my mother's and the next to the youngest of my father's. I have read books on sibling birth order and in my view, it is a curse. And even though it may be a fact because of scientific studies, it is not the Truth. What if we didn't believe in those scientific studies and tried another avenue. It's time for a transformation of thought and mind.

According to Samantha Murphy's site (http://birthorderandpersonality.com/id15.html) she utilizes other references on her "Source" tab to give detailed information about each birth child. [Her site was no longer available at the time of the publishing of this memoir. I ascertained her information in 2005]. As I looked at each child and the characteristics, I will admit it is a fact, but we are mixtures of all the groupings at certain times in different situations. What if parents prayed to seek how to raise their child and how to nurture and discipline them so their unique personality, passion and purpose were revealed? What has happened is we've raised mini-me's, lost children and children who are raising themselves. Some children maintain a sense of self, but most do not, especially first born. I was by myself for five (5) years. That was long enough to consider being an only child. And not being forewarned of an incoming sibling established how I unhealthily emotionally respond to life situations that I've fought for years. Largely not liking surprises, whether good or bad and letting go of the roles (mother, big sister, caretaker, enabler, clown) I've played not only in my family circle but life in general. I have fought tooth and nail to finally play my role, my unique, authentic role – Lana Marie Hooks. And that has been the hardest challenge of my life that I am conquering daily.

MASK/Behaviors: *Jealousy,   Envy,   Rage,   Shame,*
Repressed   Anger,   Loner,   Self-Hatred,   Selfishness,
Uncompassionate,   Victim,   Resistant   to   change,   Murderer,
Insensitivity, Attention Getter, People Pleaser, Non-Celebratory

*UNMASK: I was the only child for five years. I didn't have to
share with others unless I wanted to or I was made to. Yes, I agree
with you, I was a selfish little bald headed child, but I was five
years old. I was raised around older adults primarily being my
Mama's age (early sixties). The only time I was around kids my
age was in Kindergarten and that was half a day and even then I
was the leader who delegated to everyone what to do.*

*I wished my mother and even my Mama could have explained
to me the role of an older sister for a five year old to understand. If
they did talk to me, I can't remember what they said and by this
time I was feeling the pangs of being flawed. I have tried and
prayed, but I can only remember my sister being here and this
particular event.*

*I know hindsight is 20-20 but rage against my sister for being
alive and wanting to kill her is borderline psychotic. Yes, I can say
that because at five years of age, I showed no regard for hueman life
other than my own. I watched her go under the water and felt
nothing. I just wanted her out of my life so things could return to
normal. And that was the center of attention, negative or positive.*

*As I look at children now it scares me even more because my
generation, left with our emotional wounds unhealed, ushered in
the children of the last twenty-five to thirty years in bombing
schools, killing kids with guns, and using children as baseball bats.
It's being televised on local channels all day long.*

*This was my beginning of being resistant to change, rebellious
and a murderous heart. Change always came as a surprise and it
scared me because most changes were extreme and negative. From
that point on even in adulthood, I hated surprises, good or bad.*

*Explain to your child changes, especially major changes that
will occur in life. I don't care whether negative or positive. They*

have a right to know how their world will be affected. You can't protect them from everything. Most early traumatic changes in life are due to improper handling of life's challenges that parents and those in authority had in their early years, it's generational. They didn't know what to do or how to handle it so as adults, they are silent, used religion as a scapegoat, or scream to hide their fear and resistance to change.

I truly believe if you don't talk to your children about change, just like me they will be an insensitive five year old and an insensitive adult toward others. Teach them a balanced view on sharing even if they are an only child or first born. It is imperative that you do this. Open up their world to others who may not have what they are blessed with, but most of all, let them know that "things" can be taken away just as easily as they are given. Place the importance and value on hueman life, relationships and connecting with people.

Children are not porcelain dolls, so don't treat them as such. First born children are samples, experiments if you will. First time parents don't have any other model except themselves, so they make mini-me's out of the first born. This squashes the unique character and personality of the child and they end up, like me, searching for authenticity in later years.

First born children in certain circumstances do get more attention than the other siblings, especially if they are here for more than a year with the parent. Admittedly, I was spoiled, but I was the star for five years and that was time enough for me to believe there would be no more to share the stage with. My personality and way of thinking was set in motion. No other phenomenon or program had infiltrated to let me know that there could be another person to share with in my life. If I wasn't the center of attention, it didn't matter to me. And the greatest shame I have carried pretty much all my life is I tried to be sensitive to others but deep down I only cared about myself and I wanted others to see my pain and fix it, fix me. I didn't realize this revelation until life's experiences as a full grown woman, but emotionally a little girl and getting brutally honest with myself to

67

face the mask(s) I wore. It hurt like hell to admit these things to myself, but that was the only way I could be free to release the shame, forgive myself, others, and learn to love.

Your Memories of
Pictures, Snapshots, or
Fragments
(Write, Draw, Doodle,
Color, Scribble)

*To my brother, James, who has grown by leaps and bounds. When you came into my life I knew you and Kim were going to be a part of my life. But emotionally at the age of six there were so many things happening to me that I couldn't explain until I was an adult and demanded from God some answers about my life. I was a rejected soul that needed to go back and see where I lost my authenticity. That is why I wrote my memoir. If I can help one person then what I've gone through was worth it. I love you and am so proud of you. *

7

I'm Black and I'm Proud

The year was 1968, I'm six years old, the month is September and in a couple of weeks I will have another surprise, a baby brother. By this time I knew I would never be alone again. My breathing became shallow. I only allowed to exhale a full breath when I felt comfortable and that was usually by myself or away from home. And in a couple of weeks I would be starting first grade at Frederick Douglas Elementary School.

It was an all-Black school with Black teachers and a female Black principal named Mrs. Jones. She spoke with such authority; diction and power like Maya Angelou that it made you want to imitate her, not out of mocking but out of Black pride. Her height was almost six feet without heels and when she walked down the hallway; her steps were sure and purposed. Mrs. Jones did not allow any of her students to walk with their heads hanging down towards the floor. She would ease up beside you and tap you on your shoulder inquiring why your head was bowed. Of course, as kids we didn't know why and she would say to us, "My point exactly. There is no reason for your head to be bowed. You are a proud Black student at Frederick Douglas Elementary School." With those words coming from her mouth you had no choice but to lift up your head and walk proudly.

My teacher was Mrs. Rogers. She was a beautiful, fair skinned woman with deep auburn colored hair. It was styled in a Mary Tyler Moore flip. She wore bright white cat eye glasses, and a neon red lipstick and a small mole on the upper left side of her lip. It's amazing that I can remember her with such detail and clarity. I remember in college (twenty years later) I was researching old **Ebony** magazines when they were 11x16 and her family was in an advertisement. The late sixties advertisement portrayed her family gathered together in a wholesome setting. Her clothes, shoes and accessories looked like a model. Need I say more about her beauty, she was in **Ebony** who cast the most beautiful bouquet of men and women of that era.

Mrs. Rogers was not only beautiful, but extremely intelligent. She always taught her students on two levels. The grade that you were in and also the next level grade as well. There was no question in her book that you weren't passing to the next grade not knowing what to expect. It was a pride in teachers that when they passed you to the following grade you already knew the work required in that grade. Mrs. Rogers utilized students who caught on more quickly to assist other students who needed more time. It was like watching a hostess waltz around the room to make sure all her guests were comfortable and served properly. She was truly ahead of her time.

Now she had her discipline side as well, and could wield a paddle with the best of them. But the paddle was only used in extreme cases. She could think of other ways to discipline you and truthfully those ways hurt a lot more. For Mrs. Rogers to not allow me to assist the other students with their lessons or helping her with projects was a crushing blow to me. I couldn't take her rejecting me. I needed her attention so I could exhale a full breath.

I wanted to be just like Mrs. Rogers, beautiful and intelligent. I wanted to teach like her, dress like her, and act like her. Little did I know that the summer of 1969, I would be moving to the east side of Gary, Indiana. Another surprise? When my mother came to pick me up on the last day of school she informed Ms. Jones and Mrs. Rogers I wouldn't be returning the following year. They told my mother if things didn't work out at the new school, I could come back and be educated at Frederick Douglass Elementary School. I wished they had left me in the safe, loving arms of Frederick Douglass where respect for self and others were exemplified. They were my sheroes!

MASK/Behaviors: People Pleasing, Insatiable Need for people to like me, Overachiever, the Little Helper, Perfect Girl, Shallow Breathing, Fear of Surprises

UNMASK: PAY ATTENTION! It is imperative that you pay attention to what your child naturally gravitates to and what really interest them. If presented and exposed to different environments they will enthusiastically show and tell you their interests. This is when you must encourage your child, not dogmatically, but allow them to lead you as you open them up to options and interests. Prayer is essential because it will focus you to the places and people that will assist in bringing their gifting and talents forth. This is your child's emotional well-being, purpose and destiny at stake. You can save your children years of wandering in the wilderness trying to find out what they like, who they are, and being comfortable around people who are to help them get to where they need to be.

Mrs. Rogers and Ms. Jones showed me what I liked and it was teaching. Not just an ordinary teacher, but one who sees the uniqueness of a child and accepts nothing but excellence in them. And excellence comes in many forms, but you must be open to see it. Creativity is paramount in the field of teaching and that is what Mrs. Rogers showed me. The foundation of her learning environment was to treat each other with the utmost respect. Ms. Jones taught me to walk with my head high, take pride in my race, education is the key to freedom, speak with clarity and focus, and aim high that way your head is never bowed for no reason except in giving thanks.

I wish that philosophy had time to embed itself in my soul because I would need it living on the east side of Gary, Indiana.

8

More Dead People, a New Friend and Wet Dreams

Well, we moved on up to the east side and it wasn't a good piece of the pie contrary to *The Jefferson's* theme music. It was the first home my Mama's children all lived in since they were young. Seven people lived in a four bedroom, one and half bathroom, living room, dining room, basement, large backyard and enclosed porch home. I slept in Mama's room. Our room was where the past owner of the home died in.

One night I couldn't sleep. The house was unusually dark and quiet. Normally someone was up because I could hear them moving around, but not that night. I looked over at my Mama and she was fast asleep, snoring, making those funny sounds through her mouth. Out of the corner of my eye a figure was walking out of our closet. I wanted to move closer to Mama but I was glued to my mattress. He never turned around to look at us. He kept walking out our door, into the hallway, and then he turned right to step on the platform that led upstairs. A minor creaking of the stairs indicated nothing hueman just a possible settling of the house's foundation. I never moved for fear he would come back down the stairs to kill me.

The next morning my mother asked me did I come up the stairs the night before? I told her no. The subject didn't come up again until much later when my mother mentioned she heard and saw someone walk pass her door. [As a side note when she moved to Atlanta she always saw dead people walking around or outside our home.] It was then I told her what I saw or who I saw come out of the closet. Mama, my mother and I talked about the dead still roaming the earth, but not in depth, not the real questions I felt just beneath the surface waiting to be asked. It was never mentioned again, at least not in my presence.

Our community was diverse in culture. There were Greeks, Jamaicans, Polish, Puerto Ricans and Blacks. Another Black family had moved in the same time ours did. They had a daughter my age and I was so happy because my brother and sister were five and six years younger than me and they mainly played with each other or at times I was forced to let them play with me. So I was overjoyed for someone my age to play with.

We lived at the end of our block where we got along but the beginning of our block did not get along with us at all. In fact, we couldn't even go to the neighborhood store without an adult escort. This was my initial exposure to racism. A southern Caucasian lady would let loose her dogs on us. It was funny that her dogs only barked at the Black kids. Any other race they remained quiet. For comfort and protection several of us walked together because that was the way to school in the morning. We bonded whether it was due to strength in numbers or scared of her, but I would like to believe that we really liked being with one another.

The school I attended was larger than Douglas Elementary school. I was in second grade and for the first time I had a Caucasian teacher. She was nice, but she wasn't Mrs. Rogers. There was a boy in my class who could have been Terrance Howard, the actor's twin. The only difference was the color of his eyes. They were light brown; almost amber if you will, and they sparkled to match his even teeth smile. Every girl liked him, but as little boys are they only wanted to hit the girls and make them cry. I used to walk behind him and his mother when she came to pick him up from school. Was I a grade school stalker? If I was, put me in jail and throw away the key. This boy was F-I-N-E!!! I found myself staring at him in class and his friends teased him saying how a fat girl liked him. But I caught him staring at me in class when no one was looking. I knew he liked me as I him, but I also knew at this age, I possibly may be his friend or big sister but never the girlfriend. Anyone I liked who was handsome, cute, nice looking would have to be done in secret under the guise of darkness. I just knew that those types of boys or men didn't like fat girls or women. Sadness came over me like none other when that thought went through my mind and it lingered for a while. I knew this would be a way of life for me and I accepted it. I accepted whatever came with the price of being fat and existing in darkness. I went to bed that night and dreamt about this young Terrance Howard look alike.

I was in my backyard and he came over to play with me. Our sidewalk right by the back door was cut into three sections and one of the cement blocks led to a secret underground hideaway. I pressed on the block and it opened up to a beautiful harem palace. It was decorated with colorful scarves and huge fluffy pillows that served as furniture. I held his hand as we went through the maze of scarves. We finally came to an open space surrounded by pillows that formed a bed. I lay on the pillows and invited him to lie on top of me. He did. But something was wrong with this dream, I wasn't fat!!! I was a smaller size and he was kissing me and putting his hands on my tunecy.

I woke up to my Mama's voice telling me it was time to get ready for school. My body was hot and I felt a tingling sensation between my legs. I put my finger in my tunecy,

76

that was the name my family called the vagina, and it was wet. I was scared, but intrigued at the same time. I knew something was not right, but what was wrong? I would figure it out like a Nancy Drew mystery. Damn, it felt good when my fingers touched the insides of my tunecy.

I washed, dressed, and quickly ate my breakfast. My Mama handed me my lunch and I was off to school and my thoughts about the dream. I lagged behind my friends to figure out the connection between the dream, the tingly feeling, and my tunecy being wet. I rehashed the dream over and over in my head and each time his hand touched my tunecy the tingly feeling came over me that made the palm of my hands literally ache. Not in an ill sort of way, but an ache that if I touched them my tunecy would throb even more. I felt that warm feeling invade me from the top of my head to the soles of my feet and the wetness came like clockwork. All day at school, I repeated the dream so I could feel that warm sensation. It made me feel good about me, like I was really beautiful and wanted by every boy. Most of all it made feel that I was not fat. Seeing myself as a regular size girl in that dream showed me I was not supposed to be fat. This dream for years haunted my every waking moment to try and lose weight to get to that size. And my heart longed for and hurt after every failed diet, pill, and exercise craze. I didn't understand why I couldn't lose the weight to become the person in my dream. It was not until years later I understood why I couldn't' lose weight, which again is another book.

When I was or felt *alone, rejected, shamed, embarrassed, loud talked, and abandoned* I resorted to fantasizing. I made up stories in my head about boys/men who wanted me and I was the beautiful girl/woman that every boy/man needed. I didn't physically need a boy/man to be in my life. My stories gave me all the pleasure and company I needed. In my

77

stories I was never rejected or fat. This behavior led and enhanced to activities such as masturbation, pornography, creative lying, an introvert, and murderous thoughts to harm people who verbally or physically hurt, shamed or embarrassed me in any way. I read strong sexual content and lived my life vicariously through these fictional characters. I didn't need a person to fulfill anything for me, especially in the sexual arena. My stories included the boys/men I liked at school, in the movies, television, those I saw on the street, or in books. It didn't matter where. What mattered was I was larger than life and better than anyone around me. I think this is the opportune time to introduce you to the initiator of these stories, *Fantasy*.

Fantasy is an unseen, yet powerful negative force of the misbegotten, abused and forgotten children. Watch out for her. She will lull your child's soul to sleep to deceptively protect them from their painful place called reality. She will tell your child half-truths which are all *Lies* and they need no one but her. *Fantasy* is likened unto a hallucinogen that makes one think that everyone is against them. She is deadly because she amplifies the voices of other relatives in her family. *Self-pity, victim, pride, arrogance, false pride, false humility, denial, attention getting, false bravado, liar, hurt, anger, jealousy, competition, comparing, verbal/physical abuse*, etc. Anything that keeps a person isolated and away from REALITY, especially the traumatized, this is *Fantasy's* web. This was my life. Why? I was consistently and constantly told, embarrassed and shamed into believing that being fat I was not good enough. It didn't matter what I wasn't good for. It was the fact that I was fat. I felt I was an abomination to God and man. But later I would be introduced to another level and friend of *Fantasy*. This fiend would come into my life off and on for years until I confronted *Fantasy*. Keep reading.

MASK/Behaviors: Introverted,   Isolation, *Fantasize, Extreme Daydreamer, Masturbation, Showed a strong dislike for those in authority, Creative liar, Hated reality*

UNMASK: *Speak words of life to your children. So what if they are fat, skinny, big head, tall, short, wide, pigeon toed, bowlegged, bad skin, light skin, dark skin, nappy hair, curly hair, straight hair, biracial, or whatever. Did you ever once think they came from your seed and womb? They are miniature pictures of you. Ah! Maybe that is the reason you verbally or physically abuse them. You hate yourself? So you take it out on your child. Let's go back to the source. You were treated the same way and probably before you the same words were spoken to your parents and so on and so on. Don't you think it should stop now? Neither you nor your child deserve or need to live in fear of being the beautiful or handsome you.*

What character, talents and skills do they possess? Are they kind, loving children? Who have we allowed to tell us what our children should look like, or, act like to be accepted? What are the traits they have in spite of what the status quo dictates? Are they healthy?

This is just a recommendation to read Psalms 139 all of it, but especially verse 14 it states, "Body and soul (mind, will, emotions) I am marvelously made" (The Message Bible). After reading those passages, please listen to Mary J. Blige's CD, Growing Pains, *and listen to her joint "Work That." If that doesn't reinforce that scripture, I don't know what else does.*

Please, I implore you to start paying attention to your behavior and thoughts. Work on those emotions and behaviors that you know were someone else's reality. Start loving you so you can love your child because if you don't Fantasy will, and I guarantee she will leave her mark of Cain on them. Look at the Columbine massacre, turn on CNN and look at the news, look at teachers getting beat up by Kindergarten students. Fantasy is leaving her mark and it's getting worse. The porn industry is booming with younger and younger girls and boys. The teenage homeless issue

79

and the slave trafficking in cities such as Atlanta are growing by leaps and bounds. The internet is prime isolated time for anyone to appeal to a young girl or boy whose esteem is so low they can't see it but a predator can smell it across the broadband. It's taken me over forty years to accept and love myself, the person God made me to be (and some days I still wrestle but not as much). Don't let it be that long for you or your child.

Your Memories of
Pictures, Snapshots, or
Fragments
(Write, Draw, Doodle,
Color, Scribble)

9

Fantasy Deserves an Encore

Fantasy deserves another chapter because she is extremely cunning. She can invade any area of your life that has been traumatized by negative words and actions. Her job is to keep your soul asleep in her lair. But her invitation is the words of *Shame* that have developed from an entrenched belief system consistently spoken by *Rejected* significant people or those in authority in your life. I must take a historical pause to inject African American history where the greatest *Shame* tactics were utilized against a race of people. I know you're wondering what does this have to do with *Fantasy*. As with my grandfather's emotional battle with his enslavement and paternal lineage and self-love this has everything to do with self-love for African American people here in America. The deception *Fantasy* implemented during slavery is still in effect for those who have not awakened.

"Historically, through extreme subjugation physical differences have been utilized through shameful words and actions to produce *fear, distrust and envy for control purposes,*" [italics mine] according to the Willie Lynch Letter. Those methods were strategically used to destroy an ancient esteem, self-love, and emotional intelligence from returning to its authentic, healthy state in the family, religious institutions, educational system, the media & entertainment industry. These were systematically targeted because these are the foundations of a culture. The dysfunctional mentality that has continued to breed low self-esteem in its many forms if not faced and thought processes not transformed will continue to result in sickness and dis-ease. But the victimizer cannot help but be affected by their methods. It becomes a perverted song and dance between the victim and the victimizer because *Fantasy* is no respecter of person.

African Americans have battled with size, color of skin, and sociopoliticalreligious status since slavery. The tactics used to keep us apart were so brutal and demeaning that until this day we are still fighting to free our minds. I encourage you to read the letter in its entirety to see how a well thought out demonic plan is still in operation today. I will insert just a portion for this memoir sake.

In my bag here, I HAVE A FULL PROOF METHOD FOR CONTROLLING YOUR BLACK SLAVES. I guarantee every one of you that if installed correctly IT WILL CONTROL THE SLAVES FOR AT LEAST 300 HUNDREDS YEARS. My method is simple. Any member of your family or your overseer can use it. I HAVE OUTLINED A NUMBER OF DIFFERENCES AMONG THE SLAVES; AND I TAKE THESE DIFFERENCES AND MAKE THEM BIGGER. I USE FEAR, DISTRUST AND ENVY FOR CONTROL PURPOSES. These methods have worked on my modest plantation in the West Indies and it will work throughout the South. Take this simple little list of differences and think about them. On top of my list is "AGE" but it's there only because it starts with an "A." The second is "COLOR" or shade, there is INTELLIGENCE, SIZE, SEX, SIZES OF PLANTATIONS, STATUS on plantations, ATTITUDE of owners, whether the slaves live in the valley, on a hill, East, West, North, South, have fine hair, course hair, or is tall or short. Now that you have a list of differences, I shall give you an outline of action, but before that, I shall assure you that DISTRUST IS STRONGER THAN TRUST AND ENVY STRONGER

THAN ADULATION, RESPECT OR ADMIRATION. The Black slaves after receiving this indoctrination shall carry on and will become self-refueling and self-generating for HUNDREDS of years, maybe THOUSANDS. Don't forget you must pitch the OLD black Male vs. the YOUNG black Male, and the YOUNG black Male against the OLD black male. You must use the DARK skin slaves vs. the LIGHT skin slaves, and the LIGHT skin slaves vs. the DARK skin slaves. You must use the FEMALE vs. the MALE. And the MALE vs. the FEMALE. You must also have you white servants and over- seers distrust all-Blacks. But it is NECESSARY THAT YOUR SLAVES TRUST AND DEPEND ON US. THEY MUST LOVE, RESPECT AND TRUST ONLY US. Gentlemen, these kits are your keys to control. Use them. Have your wives and children use them, never miss an opportunity. IF USED INTENSELY FOR ONE YEAR, THE SLAVES THEMSELVES WILL REMAIN PERPETUALLY DISTRUSTFUL. Thank you gentlemen." (thetalkingdrum.com/wil.html)

Before that long Trans-Atlantic boat ride to the United States in 1619 each country on the African continent appreciated and esteemed their culture and all what makes up that region. This is not to say wars, battles, disagreements between regions were not fought. But it wasn't to destroy a culture or one's esteem; it was for others, compared to slavery in America, huemane reasons.

African people's captured and brought to the United States have been fighting a mindset that if we don't take time to search within to find the culprit naturally and spiritually, we will never know who we are and perish as a people. Many Caucasians as well are operating out of a mindset that is entrenched in the Willie Lynch plan as well. Both mindsets need to be healed. And once Truth reveals the murderer of your soul, repent for having held onto it for so long,

84

renounce everything you've done to not only hurt yourself but others and forgive yourself and others and your past generations as well. Ask Truth to guide you into being healed. Truth will – lovingly, if you accept the path to forgiveness.

Fantasy has deeply infiltrated our hueman community. We can't open a magazine without images that appear to be perfect. Young girls and boys are trying to imitate those images by any means necessary. Bulimia, anorexia, steroids, and now extreme plastic surgery by reputable or sham surgeons to get that "look." Body Image Distortion in our young females and males is growing by leaps and bounds. The media and entertainment industry show male and females posing and dressing provocatively. Teenagers are following the same trend while sexually transmitted diseases are skyrocketing, date rape; internet violations, human trafficking, and pregnancy are in raging numbers. And religious institutions are preaching at the people while behind closed doors using God as a scapegoat to molest boys and girls to satisfy their own perverted lust.

Ethnic groups that come to the United States have their own way of eating, behaving, interacting, and physical aesthetic. But not long after living here they adapt to the pervasive culture and lose theirs. Why? Educational institutions allow the "influential" to set the standard for all groups, thereby classifying those who may learn differently as ADD/ADHD, average and slow to keep a certain group of people at the top and the rest on the bottom. Detention and jail cells are being built ten to twenty years in advance predicting from low academic achievement how many males and females will be incarcerated. I left the family for last because it begins with the family and everything else follows.

It is a domino effect. Everything you learn about life starts with the family. If family members are traumatized and scarred by words, physically molested by known or unknown hands or their voice stripped by physical or emotional abuse *Fantasy* moves in to offer false relief, a haven of supposed rest and counterfeit love. If not dealt with and healed, inevitably generations of families will continue to carry *Rejection, Shame, Hurt* and *Pain* and pass these belief systems to their children.

You may also become a magnet or target for people who have not been healed of **their** shame. Unfortunately, these people are not only in our families, but our ethnic groups, religious organizations, educational institutions and media, etc. They hide behind familiarity or habit. Making excuses like "Well this is how I've always been," and, "I'm just being me and if you don't like it..." Ethnic groups say, "I grew up with everyone in my culture acting like this, it is normal for us." Religious institutions say, "If you leave this church God won't bless you" or "if you don't pay your tithe the Lord won't hear your prayers." Educational institution say, "He/She must be slow because numbers on test scores don't lie, they can't lie, numbers just don't lie." And lastly, media & entertainment justifies the industry by saying, "Sex sells and these people are grown and they can do what they want to do. I'm not bending anyone's arm to show a little t & a."

That is what *Fantasy* thrives off of. Other demeaning statements are "If you looked like...", "If you were half as smart as you are dumb", "You can't learn to ride a bike or roller skate because you are fat," "You shouldn't eat that food or you will get fat and have bad skin," "You so black," "You white looking," "High yella', " "You so skinny," "Why don't you act like a girl?", "Why don't you act like a boy and play football instead of always reading a book?", "You can sing but you don't sound like...", or "Why can't you act like...." You get the picture I'm sure. Comparing and unhealthy competition of your child with another one breeds *Self-hatred, Jealousy* and *Contempt.* This is *Fantasy's* nutrition. She loves these types of scenarios because she can really feed you more false images and words that sound so much like the Truth.

Her ally and gatekeeper is *Rejection* who will use its arsenal of children to keep a child's mind in bondage. They are *Loneliness, Self-pity, Misery* and she does love company, *Depression, Despair, Hopelessness, Suicide or Death in general.* These are *Foreboding* entities to deal with. You will appear as the victim and never the victor in your eyes. And that is the mission of *Fantasy* to keep one as a victim – forever. It is a dead zone. No living thing can ever live in the light with that mentality. She slithers around whispering words and scenes in your mind of people who more than likely did hurt and abuse you. She doesn't want you to forget them, nor the pain that caused the wound in your soul. You think everyone is against you and it produces *Smugness*, a *Self-righteousness* of sorts. Because you have been hurt, you think you deserve special attention and also a license to hurt back. Your world is myopic, small, *Selfish* and always isolated from the living.

Fantasy loves all the scenario's and excuses that are given because she knows if people are *Hurt* by their past in any shape, form or fashion, she will always have front row seat in their thoughts as she sings the siren song called *Victim* to keep the Soul (mind, will, emotions) asleep.

And while we are on the subject of sleep, remember the other fiend I mentioned at the end of the last chapter? Well, this fiend came when I was having an out of body experience. You may know of what I speak of if I describe the experience. You know when you are falling asleep and all of a sudden you feel trapped in your own body? You can see but can't blink or move. You hear and feel something moving, a sound; breathing in your face. Lying on top of you is a weight that won't move by your will or force. Your body responds as if you are having sex. It is moving, gyrating and you know this is not natural. You want to scream, but you can't, you want to holler out Jesus' name but your lips won't move. So you think the name of Jesus or the Lord's Prayer or whatever you can remember about God and it leaves, the weight leaves. I woke up feeling violated each time this happened to me. My grandmother called it "a witch riding your back." But later, much later I found out it was a demon called an *Incubus* that attacks females in their sleep. Its counterpart is called a *Succubus* that attacks males in their sleep and contrary to the definition below it is not folklore. It is real.

SUCCUBUS - In folklore, a female [devil] thought to have sexual intercourse with sleeping men.

*INCUBI - [Demonic sexual attacks on females; may be caused by **sexual sins, witchcraft spells, curses of lust, inherited curses, can attack children** (bold type my emphasis)*

SUCCUBI - demonic sexual attacks on males may be caused by the same as Incubi above (http://www. jesus-is-lord.com/incubus. htm).

The Incubus from teenage until my late twenty's would come to me and touch my breast, lay on me or would get real close to my face just barely touching my nose and breathe. But the door was created for him when I dreamed of having sex with the Terrance Howard look alike in second grade. The door opened each time I read or looked at pornographic

88

materials and masturbated (every time I got a chance). Also, due to my excessive fantasizing I summoned him to walk through the door. It's like in vampire movies you have to invite him/her in your home in order for them to bite you. Well, strong and consistent sexual fantasies, masturbation and later my curiosity lured other sexual paraphernalia in until the Incubus came when I least expected it. But usually its presence came after I fantasized after being verbally or physically traumatized by someone's words or actions toward me. As you can see there is one for the male as well. It's an equal opportunity employer. Ladies and gentlemen, this is *Fantasy* and her evil companions. TAKE HEED AND CLOSE OPEN DOORS!

10

In The West I Saw Respect, In the East I Became a Beast

Attending an all-Black elementary school with a Black principal I saw a standard of respect for self and others. In collaboration with that teaching was my Mama's biblical lesson of "turn the other cheek." In essence, don't fight, it's wrong, just walk away. That was easier said than done. Moving to the east side was a different ball game. At Frederick Douglass we wore dresses not pants unless it was winter time. I wore dresses that came from select boutiques and were hand washed not thrown in a washing machine. The east side wore Keds, earth shoes and jeans. I was dressed like a little lady, but all that was about to change.

Abraham Johnson was one of those boys you'd wished to God would've shut up and gone away. He was the class clown and instigator that knew how to manipulate bullies to not get beat up and preyed on the quiet kids to appear strong to the bullies. To me he was a nuisance that my life could have done without.

On my way home every day, and I do mean every day, he was either trying to kiss a girl like my friend Regina and hit a girl like me. I came home daily with a footprint on the back of my dress. Yes, his footprint became a designer label on my behind that my mother cussed and fussed to wash out nightly in the stationary tubs in the basement. One night highly pissed, my mother called me downstairs. I didn't know what to expect, but I knew it wasn't good. Cigarette propped in the much used gold plated ashtray now blackened by years of use sat on the old wooden detergent shelf. Her arms elbow deep in Woolite and water my mother turned around and looked me square in the face."I pay too damn much for these dresses for you to come home with a footprint on your behind. Now, if I have to come home tomorrow to a footprint on your butt, then I will whip *your* butt (She didn't use the word "butt"). Do you understand?" I knew she was serious because her teeth were clenched together the entire time, her eyes never left mine and her cigarette had burnt down to the butt.

I told her that the kids over here dressed in pants and white Ked gym shoes and if I didn't want to get beat up I'd have to dress the same way. She understood and knew times were changing so she agreed to take me shopping at the Sears & Roebuck department store, in the chubby section. But her warning still stood about me coming home with another footprint on my behind.

The next day it was raining like cats and dogs. I wished I didn't have to go to school that day, but not in my household. Come rain or shine, sleet or snow you went to school unless you were near death. My Mama handed me the bubble umbrella. For those who are not familiar with that type of umbrella, it covered you down to your waist, so the rain hits your thighs, legs and feet. At school it was the normal routine. Abraham Johnson was acting the king fool and making jokes at my expense. You would think him calling me fat would get old and stale but he would find a new way to put a spin on it. Abraham would run up beside me and pretend like I bumped him and he would thrust his body across the room as if I did it. I endured his hurtful humor daily not saying anything and if I did, it wouldn't have the desired effect as his humor did on me. He was

91

always trying to impress the class bullies James Mims and Jerome Forrest. It was really more of trying to keep them from kicking his butt.

It was still raining like cats and dogs when school ended. I tried to leave before Abraham had the chance to follow me home. He lived across the street from me next to another corner store. I was half way home when all of a sudden I felt a foot press into the umbrella into the crack of my butt. I thought I was looking out to see if I saw him come up behind me, but my vision in the rain disproved me. He kicked me so hard that I almost fell, but I managed to stay on my feet. He laughed like the Joker on Batman. I kept walking. He kicked me again. I bowed my head, afraid to retaliate. When I looked up, standing in the door with the black barbershop cow hide razor belt was my mother, swinging it like a pendulum. I knew the s#!t had hit the fan. Either my a$s was going to get whipped or I was going to whip Abraham's a$s.

I turned around to face him, folded the umbrella and used it to beat the car boiled crap out of Abraham. Needless to say the umbrella could not be used anymore and my hair, which was hot combed to make it straight went back to "can'tcha, don'tcha" stage, but it was all worth it to see Abraham bruised from head to toe and the smile on my mother's face. She and I both knew that would be the last footprint on those beautiful dresses, but more importantly not on my behind. I went to bed with a smile on my face. Something inside me changed. I knew the next day at school would be different, a turning point. I just didn't know how much.

I felt great when I woke up! I prepared for school and wore my dress and Oxford shoes. My heart felt lighter and at peace. I walked to school with pep in my step and a smile on my face. As soon as I turned the corner to enter the playground I was approached by James Mims, the class bully. He asked me did I beat up Abraham. I told him, "Yes." He said, "So you think you are bad now, huh?" I told him, "No. I just wanted him to stop kicking me." I asked him how he found out about the fight. It was after school by my house and James lived in the opposite direction. He said Abraham was going around telling everyone that I fought him back. Also, he had a bruise on his face from my umbrella.

My chest poked out a little bit and a new found boldness came upon me. By the end of the day everyone was talking about me being a bad (which means good) fighter. Bravado, toughness, bad girl, fighter all covered me like coats. I went from chubby (I was really chubby not fat) rejected girl to chubby accepted bad girl. I thought people would leave me alone, but to tell you the truth it got worse. Upperclassmen were testing me to see if I could really fight. I started fighting after school, at lunch, on the playground, everywhere. I didn't want to fight; I just wanted to be left alone. But in order for that to happen, I had to fight. The beast from the east had emerged. I preyed on people weaker than me to keep up my image. I became like Abraham. I perpetuated a lie; I didn't want to be this way, I thought. But deep down inside it made me feel powerful and good to be noticed for something other than being fat (chubby) or weak, I was strong and invincible.

MASK/Behaviors: I preyed on people weaker than me, Attention Seeker, False Bravado, Looked up to, Bully, the life I was living was a lie, Proving myself

UNMASK: False Bravado became one of the biggest mask I wore throughout elementary school and I hated it. It took so much out of me to keep this up. I just wanted to be one of the girls, have fun and for boys to like me. I wanted people to accept me for who I was and we all get along. This was the beginning of a tiresome, weary battle until my junior high school years. I hated to fight and even until this very day I still don't like to fight. And constantly trying to prove myself to people who didn't like me or if they did like me, they tested my intellect, to see how fast I could think on my feet, or see what I had to offer them to fit in. It is the most stupid thing in the world to 'test' people. But yet, this is what I had to do to survive or at least feel a part of "normal" life.

If your child comes home on a consistent basis with marks on their body or telling you about another child who is harming them, intervene quickly. Give your child reasonable advice. I do understand why my Mama told me not to fight, but I had to do something or I really believe Abraham would have kicked my uterus out. My mother did end up speaking with his mother about his behavior, and yes, his mother tried to blame it on me, but deep down she knew her son was not wrapped too tight.

Presently parents are fighting and killing other parents over their children. It is a different time and age, but something must be done to settle the differences between children and every parent must face that their child is not so innocent. Kids will fight, but as adults you must listen to them, talk to them and pray to see how to guide your child so they won't put on an unnecessary mask to survive and live a lie.

Your Memories of
Pictures, Snapshots, or
Fragments
(Write, Draw, Doodle,
Color, Scribble)

11

Prayer Changes Things?

Leaving the womb of my mother, I landed in my Mama's arms and that meant being in church. She had a key to every door to the church so I didn't have a choice but to be there. Each auxiliary meeting to prayer meeting on Wednesday night I attended them all, but prayer meetings were the ones I watched in awe and fear. These ladies testified and prayed with fervency around that altar to heaven moved and hell froze. I saw the power of God move mightily and heavily as tears fell, and doilies on their heads, and long sleeve, ankle length white dresses were soaked in sweat.

They had a list of names in which they called out prior to gathering around the altar to pray. Some people I knew and others I had no clue of who they were. But it didn't matter whether you were a member of the church or not. If your name was on that list, you were prayed over. I saw my Mama pray at church with the same zealousness at home at 3:00 a.m. It was no different. She even had a room in the basement of the house designated as her prayer room. Over the door was a sign that stated, "Prayer changes things, if you desire prayer enter in." Sometimes I would sit in her rocking chair in our bedroom, get real quiet and listen to her "go before the Lord." She would start out singing "Jesus Loves Me" followed by "Jesus Keep Me Near the Cross." I knew after that song she was on her knees to begin praying. The hours she would travail before the Lord and call out family member names and friends to Him astounded me. I was even privy to seeing some of those people come to her for prayer. She never once denied any person who asked for prayer. My uncle's friends who drank like fish out of the water came to her with liquor on their breath asking for prayer. She did tell them about their drinking but did not deny them prayer. Her constant reminder to each person after prayer was "prayer changes things." I listened to her say this line as if her life depended on it. I had a need, a major need in me that prayer needed to change. I believed that if my Mama knew that "prayer changes things" then it had to change something for me.

It was getting close to the end of the school year. Next year I would be in third grade and I wanted my life to be different. *I* wanted to be different. I recognized and understood the vast difference in body sizes. That entire year from being called "Bertha Butt" (song by The Jimmy Castor Bunch), to the song "Bump No Mo' with No Big Fat Woman" I knew I did not look like other girls in my class, especially my neighbor Regina. Certain relatives compared my size to hers, also how neat she was, and the ladylike way she carried herself. I thought that if that is what pleased them, then maybe, if God answered my prayer, my family would like me.

I was getting ready for bed and my Mama reminded me to pray before I got into it. I got on my knees and said the *Lord's Prayer.* My Mama told me I was getting too old to just say that prayer. I could add more to my prayers. I knew I was going to say more, I just didn't want her to hear what I was praying. I crawled into bed, closed my eyes and said the words in my head.

God, I want to be small like Regina. I want to wear clothes like her so my family will like me. Now my Mama says, "prayer changes things," *so you have to answer my prayers. Please change me by the time I wake up in the morning. I want to be small. Thank you.*

I went to bed knowing and believing that by morning I was going to have a new body. God answered the praying women at church and he answered my Mama's prayers, so He had to answer mine too.

The next morning my Mama told me to get up and get ready for school. I didn't open my eyes. I wanted the new me to be a surprise. I knew my Mama saw the new me, she just didn't want to spoil my surprise. I took my hand and began to feel my stomach. It felt the same. I thought maybe God started with my legs and it would be a gradual change each night. Again, my Mama called my name again to get up and get ready for school. I refused to open my eyes- yet. I slowly moved my hand to my outer left thigh. It wouldn't have far to go to get to my inner thigh – I thought. Moving my hand inch by inch I probed to see if any changes had been made. I stopped. Bending my leg toward my stomach I opened my left eye and saw the brown mole in the middle of my left thigh, my chubby thigh. I was extremely hurt that there was no change whatsoever to my body. The tears came before I could stop them. God didn't answer my prayer! Maybe He wanted me to be chubby, fat, or, my prayers weren't good enough to be answered, like the women in the church or my Mama. I wasn't good enough. I needed to prove to God, I was good enough so He would answer my prayers. I had to do everything right, everything perfect. I had to be perfect like the ladies at the Wednesday night prayer meeting and more importantly, my Mama; because she knew "prayer changes things." And I believed her believing her mantra. I just had to be like her – perfect.

MASK/Behaviors: Perfection, Drama Queen, Low Self-Esteem, Self-Hatred, Hypocrite, Body Image Distortion, Unhealthy perception of God, Jealousy, Femininity compromised

UNMASK: I really believed with everything in me that "prayer changes things." Viewing the women at church, my Mama and seeing the results of their prayers I knew mine would be answered too. And because mine wasn't answered by the same God they prayed too, I was hurt. I saw those praying women get results from God and I was jealous of that relationship. I asked God to fix several heart issues, one of which was being fat. I really wanted that prayer to be answered. And I thought if I was good that would qualify my prayers to be answered. Whatever I was asked to do in church I did. At home, I stayed out of everyone's way by watching television, a lot of television. This became my escape. I fantasized about looking like those characters and having that "Hollywood" type of life.

I believed that because I wasn't small, neat and ladylike God didn't like me. I have been trying to prove my worth to God and man all my life. I believed God endorsed my family, church members and those in the educational system to say shameful words about my weight, appearance, femininity and intellect. Being seen as less than by these three institutions defined my relationship or non-relationship with God and man. It took me years and experiencing struggle after struggle to know that being good doesn't qualify prayers to be answered.

Truth revealed why my prayer wasn't answered as I was completing this book. I don't want your child to take that long to know that they are good enough as they are, and to know that God loves them and people who call them names are ashamed of themselves. God doesn't love one person more than the other. He is no respecter of person even though sometimes it feels and looks like it. People who are ashamed of themselves are hurting and will hurt other people. They will cause division and strife out of their jealousy, anger and rage. It doesn't matter if they are in your family, church or school. In fact, if Divine Intervention doesn't help you, you will behave the same way as those who hurt you just as I did. I will continue to say this until it hits home. Hurt people, hurt people. But if you choose not to come out of your hurt, then you will, others will, continue in the same unhealthy behavior. Your beginnings don't determine your end. It's the choice you make in the middle.

Your Memories of
Pictures, Snapshots, or
Fragments
(Write, Draw, Doodle,
Color, Scribble)

12

Devil n' the Backyard and Jesus n' the Bedroom

Memorial Day, July 4th and Labor Day you could count on our house having a barbecue party. When I saw the six foot long, wood ingrained hi-fi with radio, and eight track stereo system, being hauled from the living room through the dining room, and down the kitchen steps, to the backyard with extension cords going out the back door looking like spaghetti, I knew it was on like popcorn.

My uncle had more beef, chicken and pork sacrificed to the pit god than anybody on the block. Kool filter kings, Pall Mall cigarettes, Lucky Strikes and liquid spirit were bought from the county line (a wholesale discount liquor store between Indiana and Illinois) in boxes that we were not allowed to look inside. But I, being the nosy child, would sneak downstairs to the basement and look in the freezer and refrigerator and see it stocked with Hennessy, Wild Irish Rose, Wild Turkey, Skol, E&J (affectionately I learned later it was called Erk & Jerk), Jim Beam, Canadian Club, and the old standby's Miller, Pabst Blue Ribbon, Stroh's and Budweiser. I knew once these were consumed what it would do to people's personalities. It gave them courage to speak their honest thoughts, in which they could not do sober minded. And when I looked at my Mama's face when they drank, I knew what she thought. *Lord, save my children and their friends.*

Bid Whist, Old Maid, Funk and R&B music, kickball, and Double Dutch, a jumping rope game, were played until the street lamps came on signaling for the kids to go inside their homes. At midnight the down home blues took the adults on into the early mornin'. My Mama prayed herself to sleep naming every person in the backyard for God's spirit to keep. I tried to go to sleep, but I felt guilty because I wished I were outside with the other spirit. That god seemed to be having more fun from the sound of their voices. Plus, they could stay up late and I couldn't. But then (isn't there always a but) a harsh word was spoken, an accusation made, followed by more cursing. I knew what was next. Like clockwork, it never failed, the fight, maybe a gun pulled, the sound of the back iron gate closing, a car door slamming, and Mama still praying in her sleep for the Lord to change their hearts before falling into a deep slumber. It was then she released them to the Lord's care, and I still felt guilty because I wanted to be with the devil in the back yard.

🀄 *MASK/Behaviors: Hypocrite, Afraid to enjoy myself, Afraid to laugh, Afraid to celebrate, People pleasing, Spirit of Perfection*

UNMASK: I liked when we had our backyard barbecues. The steel mill employees and some of the Lake County Department of Public Welfare employees, and neighbors were in our yard eating, dancing, playing cards and the kids were either on my swing set or playing games. But I felt guilty because of how my Mama felt about the drinking and playing cards. It was sin to her and I knew how she felt about it. And I didn't want to disappoint her so I pretended to dislike it as well.

Deep down I always wanted to go to parties growing up and on occasion when I did, I felt out of place, guilty, and plus I never was asked to dance. So I hid behind a self-righteous and a major hypocrite mask. When all I really wanted to do was dance, that's all, just dance. I could have cared less about the drinking. It was the dancing I missed.

I knew the latest dances that came out year after year. I practiced in my bedroom watching "Soul Train." We had sock hops at school and the boys didn't dance with me because I didn't fit their image. They couldn't be seen with a girl like me so I sat on the bench in the gymnasium watching, wishing and hoping that someone had the nerve to ask me to dance. And when I did dance in a girl circle, some of the girls made fun of me being chubby/fat and dancing. Sometimes they were worse than the boys. I stopped thinking about dances, parties, get-togethers, and any social gatherings. I didn't fit the image even though I could dance. I didn't want to feel left out.

Allow your child to enjoy the chaperoned parties. It's okay to dance and have fun. You set the tone for their social graces. But it needs to be done in a healthy way, a way unique to your child's gifts, destiny and purpose. Show your child it's okay to dance. Take them to see the Alvin Ailey Dance Troupe or the Dance Theatre of Harlem, or your local dance company. Dance with them around the house and dance with them in the rain. Dancing is your body singing to the beat. It's natural to want to sway to the music. David did in the bible and he partied so hard that his clothes came off.

Your Memories of
Pictures, Snapshots, or
Fragments
(Write, Draw, Doodle,
Color, Scribble)

13

A Fragment of Happiness

My third grade teacher was Mrs. Smith, a tall, smooth brown skinned, gaunt, Masai warrior-looking woman. She wore cat eyeglasses, red lipstick, and her ever present light knit sweater that never left her sharp shoulders. She was truly a product of the sixties, even though it was the early seventies. Not a very loud woman in voice, but she made up for it with her two rulers bound by tape that would meet your knuckles if you misbehaved. I felt the wrath of those rulers at least twice weekly. I was quite the talker interrupting those who were doing their work when I finished mine first. But being in her class was calming amidst what was happening to me on the playground.

On the playground my reputation for fighting grew daily. I fought old bullies and incoming new ones. Dressed in my stretch pants with the attached strap to the leg of the pant that went under your foot and white Keds gym shoes I fought to protect myself. But inwardly, the false bravado was wearing thin. I didn't like to fight. I just wanted to be accepted for me, whoever that was. I was losing the real me a little bit each day. It felt like a sculptor taking his chisel and chipping the real me down to whatever I was becoming. The public persona was a fighter, cool, good girl, intellect, and bully. The private person was depressed, oppressed, hurt, angry and wishing I was small and pretty. It was a different grade, but same s#! +.

My fourth grade teacher embodied the seventies diva warriors *Coffy and Cleopatra Jones* and the revolutionary social and political organization *The Black Panther Party* rolled into one woman. She was extremely intelligent and socially and politically conscious. Whatever her mood was it dictated her hairstyle. One day her hair would be an Afro. The next day she may have worn a bone straight wig, and the day after that a flip style. She had a wig for every occasion. I don't think I ever saw her real hair. Oh, yes I did. Her hair was natural and she wore it closely cropped to her head in a teenie weenie Afro. All the boys in the class loved when she wore miniskirts or form fitting knitted dresses. Their hormones raged out of control, but she knew how to put them back in check without embarrassing them. She was young and dedicated as any tenured teacher could ever be in the profession of teaching. And if you stepped out of line her reach for the paddle was just a hair's breath away. But she also knew how to have fun in style!!!

Christmas and Black History Week (yes, I grew up in the era of the week) were her favorite times to celebrate. Christmas was collard greens, ham, fried chicken, turkey and dressing, Kool & the Gang and the Ohio Players. We partied like you would never believe with her in the middle of the classroom dancing with us. Her partying spirit made me forget that I was chubby. We danced like no tomorrow. The "Penguin" and the "Scorpion" (much like the "Electric Slide") were the latest dances and we did it up. She chaired Black History Week every year too. That particular year she asked me to recite Langston Hughes', *The Negro Speaks of Rivers*. My mother had a red, black and green dashiki knitted for me by her friend. My hair was in an Afro and I felt like Angela Davis with her fist raised high leaving prison. I received so many compliments on my attire and greater ones on my rendition of Langston's poem. I did Langston proud that day and fell in love with his poetry too. My mother attended and I was so happy. But some people in my class didn't share that same sentiment.

There were two girls in my class that were really pretty. One looked mixed with Native American features, the other an African princess. The boys in the class treated them as if no other girls in the class existed. Being smart I thought would get me noticed, but it was not enough. Even being a fighter I thought would get me in with them at least to be around them but I fought in vain. I protected one Caucasian girl in our class named Tracy. She was so frightened of the Black girls, but she liked me as I her until one day the bully girls wanted me to hit her. And sad to say I didn't have the courage to say no. I hit Tracy and I felt so bad that when I got home my stomach lurched but I didn't vomit. I cried. Tracy never looked at me the same again.

I began talking like the cute girls and acting like them to see if I could get the same attention. It still didn't make any difference. I wasn't accepted by the boys and I was a joke to the girls. They still looked at me as the fat girl wanna be. I stopped trying. But this new mask called *imitation* I was acquiring was so easy and I was good at it. It was natural to me. I mean I felt something overtake me when I imitated not just them but anyone. I was especially good at voice overs of actors. My family all said how I became that person not only in voice inflections, but behavior and body movements. I didn't pick up on what was really being said to me until years later. Before identity theft I was stealing people's voices, personalities and sometimes character traits. Acting like someone else made my family laugh. They paid attention to me. They spent time with me without an insult or screaming at me. They actually looked at my body with a smile even though I was behaving like someone else. I thought it was a small price to pay for a laugh, for some pleasant attention. Little did I know it would cost me so much more in the end.

The next year I would be attending a new school due to the schools closing in our area. We were the first generation of "bussed kids." I wasn't quite sure which school I would attend. That information would come after the school year ended. I wished I'd stayed at Frederick Douglass Elementary School. If I had, I believe I would have had a chance for my self respect to mature. The next two years would seal the loss of respect for self and others with words that would come at me like a machine gun and my emotional bullet proof vest wouldn't stand the impact.

MASK/Behaviors: Imitation, Unhealthy Self-Image, Conformity, Joker, Bully, Comparing, Competing, Fighter, Spirit of Perfection, Liar, Hid behind Intellect, False Cool Girl, Mild Schizophrenia, Anger

UNMASK: The third and fourth grade years at Spaulding Elementary School revealed new entities and new mask to wear. Imitation became not just what I did, but I had a plethora of personas that gave me the attention I craved. I was convinced that fighting, bullying and pretending to be the cute girl was not enough to gain the attention of the cute boys.

It didn't dawn on me until I was in my thirties that imitation was not natural, especially if you don't know who you are. I started questioning my personality, the way I walked, talked, thought, even my handwriting. I know it sounds crazy, but I didn't know if anything about me was authentic. My facial expressions and gestures were they really me? Here I was in my thirties looking at myself in the mirror and I didn't have a clue as to who was staring back at me.

This is what happens when the authentic person has been rejected by consistent words of shame. Those words, if believed to the very core of one's soul will tear down a person's authenticity. Inevitably, this leads to unhealthy behavior's to survive. Schizophrenia, multiple personalities will come forth because the person's authentic personality, behavior and emotional self realize the cost is too high for her/him to come out of hiding.

Allow your child to be themselves, embrace their uniqueness, their style, their goofiness, their laugh, walk, talk, how they view the world, whomever God has made them to be. Just love them and let them be!

Your Memories of
Pictures, Snapshots, or
Fragments
(Write, Draw, Doodle,
Color, Scribble)

14

The Bug

My Mama had three good friends, but one of those three was closer than a sister to her, Ms. Taylor. DNA was not as close as Ms. Taylor and my Mama. I loved when they were on the phone. They laughed and giggled like teenagers as they talked for hours on end. It was funny how they greeted each other. Most people who know each other greet each other by first names, or nicknames, no; they called each other by their last names. They had a kind of friendship that you "lay down your life" for. They defended and protected each other. And no one else dared to negatively talk about one to the other. They had a bond I admired, revered and loved. I truly wished I had that kind of fierce, loyal friendship.

Mrs. Taylor called my Mama and told her about a senior citizen group that planned tours to different parts of the United States. She wanted my Mama and me to go with her and her granddaughter on a tour of Washington, D.C. and the surrounding areas for two weeks. I was excited when my Mama told me about the trip. She told her oldest son about the cost of the trip and how much spending money she needed. I laughed because her son was putty in her hands. It didn't take her long to sweet talk him. He'd just cough up the money. I on the other hand had to ask my father for the money and I wasn't sure what his reaction would be. All I remember was he paid for it and I was on my way to D.C. It is a blur to me as to how he responded. I just knew that it was paid for and my bags were packed before the last payment was due.

This was my first tour and I was bit by the traveling bug. I enjoyed being with the senior citizens. They were funny as all get out. Their stories of yesteryear were entertaining. But what I enjoyed was their gossip about every big pastor in Gary, Indiana and what was going on behind their closed doors. They talked about the soap operas, their children and husbands. It was hilarious. I sat for hours pretending to read my book while eavesdropping. Those two weeks granted me the serenity I needed.

I had so much fun, especially when we entered the White House. I was thrilled to be in the President's home. I stepped into history and it was fascinating. My Mama bought me souvenir booklets that I kept for years. Learning the history of people, places and things greatly interested me when we traveled. I knew traveling and learning about different cultures is what I wanted to do when I was older.

MASK/Behaviors: None

AUTHENTIC: The traveling bug bit me hard. I enjoyed being on the road with my elders. I learned from them by listening and watching. I'm not saying all what they said or did was correct, but experience sometimes beats age. My Mama and Mrs. Taylor had a fierce relationship that I still smile about. When they talked on the phone it was like watching teenage girls laughing and talking about the latest trend. Mrs. Taylor was like my second Mama. Her granddaughter and I were friends growing up even though I was three years older than her. We traveled together with our Mamas; in fact, we were joined at the hip like Siamese twins with them. I wished the bug of authentic friendship had bit me like our Mamas. Traveling coupled with true friendships in later years would have been a lovely marriage. But at least in this moment, no mask was

*born or worn. A love to see the world and its people were birthed in
me and that was a beautiful delivery.*

Your Memories of
Pictures, Snapshots, or
Fragments
(Write, Draw, Doodle,
Color, Scribble)

15

The Upper Room

My oldest uncle's room was between my mother's and aunt's. His room was a mystery, a place that held secrets I wanted to know about. He and his friends would congregate in there with the door closed. I heard laughter, smelled cigarettes or some other unknown smell and liquor. But I wanted to see for myself. What was so special about this room that drew men and women from the steel mills of Gary, Indiana? I was tired of imagining what possibly could be going on in the upper room.

At times he allowed me to come in if they were watching television, listening to music or talking about subjects that were tame. He had one window in his room and it was always open. Even in winter it was cracked or fully opened if people were in there. But I wanted to be in his room when no one was there and I did get my chance when my Mama, brother and sister took a nap one day during summer vacation.

The stairs creaked a bit, but I knew where to stop at for the least amount of noise. I treaded ever so lightly and once at the top of the stairs I opened his door. I left it open to hear anyone come in through the downstairs main front door or someone come up the stairs. I was in his room, the uncle I looked up to like a hero. I would later learn how he truly felt about me and the name he tagged me as.

On the left side of his bed was a metal nightstand. I saw what I thought were comic books and I loved animation. I carefully picked one up because his room was immaculately clean and in order. I didn't want him to notice anything out of place. My moves had to be delicate and precise. I saw the faces of Popeye, Olive Oil and Bluto. I picked the book up and saw the entire scene. It was a penis in Olive Oil's behind and one in her mouth. That feeling in my tunecy hit me hard. The palms of my hands pleasurably ached. I opened the book and read, no; saw more cartoons in different sexual positions. Voraciously I read what little caption they had underneath the picture, but it was the pictures my body longed for. The clear stuff was oozing out of me. I could feel it coming... "Lana, where are you at?!" I jumped a mile high off the floor."I'm upstairs in the bathroom." I carefully placed the comic book back where it was originally at. I closed his door and entered the bathroom, which was directly across from his room. I flushed the toilet and stealthily walked back down the stairs. My Mama met me at the bottom of the stairwell. "I hope you weren't in your uncle's room." That's all she said and walked away. I couldn't show any guilt in my face or body stance. I'd learned to control them quite well. This was vital if I was going to do this again. And again and again, I did. But not just his room, but my mother's as well.

Her closet held books upon books about slavery and romance. I read books about plantation life like **Mandingo** and the **Falconhurst Plantation** series that described in great detail the forbidden love of a Caucasian woman and an enslaved African man. Anything that had strong sexual content captured my attention. *Fantasy* utilized this material for me to gorge on to feed my imagination with illusions of boys treating me the same as what I read. I was hooked on pornography for years. It was a continuation on a higher level of *Fantasy*'s process to keep me living in her world. The more my weight was talked about, or peers rejected me the more I retreated to *Fantasy*'s pseudo haven. *Fantasy* knew what I needed because the pain of being rejected was becoming greater inside of me. Staying under the basement stairwell was my sanctum, my safe place. Television was my second sanctum, my escape to imagine myself as the beautiful leading lady. Imitation was my third sanctum. For a while I owned the personalities of the people I desired to be to get attention from my family. And in addition to this pseudo-family that *Rejection* and *Fantasy* was growing for me pornography was birthed in the upper room. Pornography added imagery to the storylines that not only made me the leading lady, but the vixen, and the enchantress that no man could resist. My body was flexible, voluptuous, a sexiness that I began to believe I really was. The lines were skewed in my mind. I knew the cute guys really wanted me no matter what their actions or words stated differently. I believed what I read in books, and saw on television because *Fantasy* told me it was true underneath the basement stairwell. And she was always right, right?

MASK/Behaviors: Pornography,   Isolation, Masturbation, Liar, Manipulation, Deceit, Self-Hatred, Self-Rejection, Oppressed, Self-Delusional, Control, Body Image Distortion

UNMASK: With each story I read I replaced the beautiful female with myself. Since I knew the cute boys I liked wouldn't admit they liked me (and some did) they became a part of my story. My imagination became a force that my body responded to anywhere. The only place I didn't fantasize was in church. I did respect God's house. But if someone said anything about my weight as soon as I got home from church my imagination turned on like I turned the knob on the television. This was my secret, my

118

way of being invisible so no one would see me and talk about me. I was in control of this world - I thought. No one could tell me what to do, when to do it, and how to do it. I was the story and the storyteller.

If this even sounds remotely like your child, intervene, please intervene. Search their room. They don't pay the rent or mortgage – you do. Check out what they are reading, or looking at on the internet. More importantly, what are you reading and looking at? Talk to your child and ask them what is going on in their world. I know you probably work, go to school and tired when you get home. But fifteen minutes makes all the difference in the world. Just sit and listen to your child. All they want is someone to listen and acknowledge their presence. Shouldn't it be you?

16

This Is Sheffield's Play

It was summertime and that meant jumping rope, single and Double Dutch. Regina and I played with dolls, but I really wasn't a doll person. I was more of a tomboy. Anything rough and ready I participated in, like trying to climb our yard tree and playing hide and seek.

I remember one time Regina and I were bored. We sat on my front steps moping. My Mama was standing on the porch looking at our faces through the screen window. She asked why we weren't playing. We told her we were bored and didn't have enough people to play jump rope. It was just her and me and we needed another person to turn the rope. She then started telling us about her "when I was a little girl" stories. We indulged her, but wished she'd hurry up and get to the point. I loved her, but she was long winded. A trait I picked up later in life. That's what I get for wanting her to hurry up with her stories.

The next thing we knew she told us to move away from the door so we wouldn't get hit by it as she came outside. She picked up one end of the rope and told me to get the other end. I did. My Mama turned that rope while Regina jumped to *Orange light, orange light big and round, see if you can touch the ground.* Regina jumped as long as she could then it was my Mama's turn. I was shocked! My Mama jumped her sixty plus age legs off. The more she jumped the younger, she looked. Then it was my turn. To tell you the truth, I didn't want a turn. I got a kick out of seeing my Mama jump rope. Then we played *High water, Low water*. My Mama jumped over that rope like she probably did as a young girl in Sheffield, Alabama. I mean I was happy to see her laughing as she sweated her wig to the side of her head. My younger brother and sister were running around the yard playing as well. You could feel the joy in the yard.

My other relatives came in from work, took off their clothes and joined us outside. They sat on the steps while my Mama jumped away. Afterwards we learned how to play Ball and Jacks with rocks. Granted, our hands hurt from hitting concrete, but we learned. We all stayed outside and played until the street lamps came on. Regina turned to me and said, "I hope your grandmother plays with us again tomorrow." I felt good when she said that to me. Maybe it was my Mama playing with us that day that I felt a connection with Regina. As happy as I was that day, I should have cherished it because it wouldn't be many more. The next day my Mama did play with us and she taught us other games too.

🐝 *MASK/Behaviors: People Pleasing*

UNMASK: I grew out of playing with dolls. I didn't feel like a girl. In fact, I cut the hair off my dolls. My Barbie and Chrissy dolls were cut bald within three weeks of getting them. The only doll I thoroughly enjoyed was my Julia doll. It was the character Dihanne Carroll played on television as the first Black nurse. All of her clothes were handmade by a friend of my mother's and she was my favorite doll. I'm not sure what happened to that doll, but her hair was spared.

I was a tomboy. Any activity where I could move my body, run or play board games that used my mind, was my kind of fun. It was okay to like what I liked and not join in what I didn't like. It wouldn't have made me a bad person, but I was too far gone in pleasing people to know that what I liked and thought was right for me. I feared rejection and people more so than honoring who I authentically was. I couldn't risk losing a friendship and too terrified to see if it would stand on its own. Teach your kids it's okay to respect what others like, but respect what they think, what they like, and the activities they enjoy as well.

Your Memories of
Pictures, Snapshots, or
Fragments
(Write, Draw, Doodle,
Color, Scribble)

17

Piano Lessons

The only reason I took piano lessons was because my family compared me to our cousin who could play the skin off the keys and a young lady at church who played like Mozart. I knew I would never be either one of them, nor did I want to be. I didn't know what I wanted to do but playing the piano was not it. My family did ask me did I want to take lessons, but what convinced me and made me feel guilty all at the same time was my Mama. It made her happy and I wanted her to be proud of me.

I reluctantly called my father to ask him to pay for the lessons. I could hear in his voice the hesitation of not wanting to do it. He felt that his monthly child support of sixty dollars was enough to support me. But he did pay (or made my older brother pay for them, among other things I learned as an adult) for the lessons that neither he nor I wanted.

My piano teacher was a real good friend of our family. She lived about four or five blocks away from our street. It was in walking distance and every Saturday I walked to and from her home. I didn't like to walk because the back of my legs hurt so badly. My family thought I was being lazy, but I wasn't. The back of my legs were on fire when I walked long distances. Periodically I had to stop and rest so I could relieve the pain in my legs.

One evening on the local news there was a report out about a man raping young girls. He was spotted on the west side of town, but an all-points bulletin was out for the citizens of all areas to be on the lookout and to be cautious of where their young girls walked. The following Saturday I was told to walk swiftly to my piano teacher's home and call when I arrived. When I arrived at Ms. Jessie Mae's house I called my Mama and told her I was there. The lesson went as usual. I tried to really be interested, but Ms. Jessie Mae knew I wasn't and her patience was waning with my mediocre attempts to learn how to play the piano. I knew I had some decisions to make, but I was at least going to try for several more months before I quit. Maybe, I thought, something would click in my brain to love the piano. But deep down I knew this was not my forte and Ms. Jessie Mae knew it as well. I left Ms. Jessie Mae's home wishing I had the guts to tell my family I didn't want to take piano lessons. I was already a disappointment to them by not being physically attractive and a tomboy. I had to redeem myself in some way and right at that moment piano lessons was the avenue.

I took my time walking home. I just wanted to think clearly and not be disturbed by anyone. It was hot that day too. I mean you could see the heat rising from the concrete. At first I didn't notice this car trailing me. There was an abandoned building and I stopped to look in the window. That's when I saw the car. I wanted to see if the car would continue or stop. It stopped.

"Hey," the voice spoke to me, "It sure is hot out here, ain't it?"
I turned around to address the voice. "Yes," I smiled.
I started walking back towards home. "You cute."

"Thank you," I said.

"You want a ride?" "No, I can walk. I just live on the next block." I lied. But I thought he would go away if I said I was real close to my home.

He didn't take the bait." You look tired and I can give you a ride the rest of the way."

"No, please leave me alone. I can walk."

I was almost running now. Fear was creeping into the pit of my stomach. The alley behind my street was the next plan of action to run down to my gate. Blessedly, I was the first house on the street next to the apartments on the corner.

"C'mon, I can take you home. You so cute and I know your family. They won't mind."

I took off running toward the alley and to the gate where my yard was. I thought he'd followed me, but he didn't. He kept straight. I knew the back door would be closed and locked so I opened the other gate and ran between my house and the next door neighbor, Mr. Chicks, home. I rang the doorbell frantically. My Mama came to the door, irritated by the ringing."Why are you ringing the doorbell like that?" I told her the entire story on the front porch. The only words coming from her mouth are "Oh Lord, my Lord." She told me to lie down on the couch on the porch. I fell asleep.

I woke up to cussing and pleading. My Mama told my oldest uncle and he went ballistic. Upstairs he went to the closet, the closet that held artillery like none other. Rifle in hand, he came down the stairs and walked out the front door. He marched along Eighth Avenue to announce to "the motherfucker who messes with his niece and anyone in his family, he will blow them to hell." A police car came down the street and my Mama is calling on the Lord with everything in her being. They stopped and called him over to the car. My Mama is afraid he is going to be carted off to jail. One of them gets out of the car and the other is still behind the wheel of the car. Odd, I thought. Normally both policemen get out as backup just in case the supposed offender wants to either bolt or fire. I watched enough television to know the routine. Later we find out that he knows them. They went to school together. An agreement between them is made. He can walk down the street with the rifle but he can't fire it. They turned the car around and parked in the cleaner's lot. My uncle continued to walk up and down the street with his rifle yelling at the top of his lungs saying how he will kill the motherfucker and you ain't a man when you've got to mess with little girls. The policemen are laughing their tails off because they know he will kill the man if found. After he finished his tirade he walked to the liquor store, bought him his drink of choice and walked home. The police drove away.

He walked in the house, looked down at me and smiled. John Wayne that is all I can think of. John Wayne told the whole block what he would do if anyone messed with his family, and messed with me. I felt protected, loved, wanted and worthy. Maybe I was still a part of this family after all, maybe?

MASK/Behaviors: Hypocrite, People Pleasing, Sexual Self-Harm

UNMASK: I should have been honest and told my family I didn't want to take piano lessons, but I was afraid that would be one more thing added to the list of why I wasn't good enough. I didn't want my Mama to side with them and leave me truly all alone. She was the only one who defended me and I didn't want her displeased with me. I knew I was wasting Ms. Jessie Mae's time and she did too, but I had to trudge through this until hopefully, maybe, the piano would grow on me. Guilt and fear of rejection overrode common sense and Truth.

When my uncle defended my honor, it made me feel good. Here it was a man; my family member took his rifle and walked up and down the street telling any and everyone what he would do if they tried to harm me. Wow, I thought this is what men are supposed to do for women, protect them and if a man didn't, he was a coward in my eyes.

There is a price to be true with self- first, and then to everyone else. It's confessional time. The day I walked home from piano lessons and that man approached me and said, "You're cute." For a split second I considered getting in the car with him. Why you say? This man was going to harm me if I got in the car with him. You're right. I was only nine years old and I knew his intention. But he told me I was cute, a stranger, a male, a rapist.

If I sound like a broken record, I mean to. The more you constantly demean your child's body image, color of skin, calling them out of their character, comparing them to another child, or don't protect them against significant others or those in authority, the first time a male or female approaches them and tells them they're cute, or any other words of flattery, they will either think about going with them or go with them.

If your child's esteem is shattered to the point they are willing to put their life in danger just to hear a male, a man, a woman, a female tell them words they are not used to hearing by those closest to them, this sets them up for people whose intentions could result in prostitution, human trafficking, molestation, kidnapping, cult sacrificing, and the unthinkable, murder.

When I thought about how close I came to getting in that car and why, I cried. I cried because I never thought about my mindset or, my reasoning until this writing. Every feeling came back like it was yesterday. I felt ashamed, but it explained the pattern in my relationship with men and the type of men I attracted except for two men in my entire life. But the other type of men I attracted were a totally different breed.

128

There were three types of men I attracted. The first was like the man who approached me coming from piano lessons. The kind that told you what you wanted to hear. They could smell my low self-esteem. When they touched me it started off gently then it ended up being abusive. My desperation was their elixir to treat me any way they wanted to – a mixture of verbal and physical. They knew I wasn't going to call for help or fight back. I was too scared of what they might do to me like leaving me. Before date rape was considered a form of rape, I experienced it, as well as after it was accepted as a form of rape. I stayed silent because I was too afraid and ashamed of people knowing how gullible I was. So I allowed whatever to happen to me. Through the years I did get up enough nerve to leave situations, but I had to understand why I put myself in harm's way. And it went back to the "words." These abusive men told me what I desperately wanted to hear. I was cute or they spoke to my intellect. The two things I was humiliated from those I loved and those I thought who loved me.

The second types were men who had equally low self-esteem and they were not physically appealing to pretty women. They were like me hefty, or, very small men that wanted to be accepted. These men were pushovers. I spoke to their esteem, listened to their stories of woe and built them up only to make myself feel powerful and good about me. They used terms of endearment that made me feel good about being a female, but deep down it was not the type of man I desired.

The third type was an effeminate man. No sexual involvement. I had a friendship with them that I would've liked to have had with females. These men were my confidants that I could divulge my worst secrets, and they were my Truth tellers on anything and everything. But they were hurt like I was. In fact, some of their beginnings were worse than mine. But this type of man I felt comfortable with, not threatened. I could breathe.

Look at your child right now and tell them they are smart, pretty, handsome, intelligent, you admire them, praise their scribbling work, their green elephants and gray flowers. You don't have to go overboard with your compliments and praise, but better you tell them and show them than someone who has an ulterior motive that will possibly harm them.

I had a friend raising her teenage daughter. On my visits to her home, I often heard her tell her daughter she was cute. Even if they fought and fussed they hugged, made up and loved each other even more. I eventually asked her why she told her daughter how cute she was. Her reply was, "She is cute. And when my daughter is out there and men will approach her and tell her she is cute, I want her to tell them, 'I know that because my Mama told me. Now tell me something I don't know.'" I must admit I was taken aback. But she further explained that, "Sometimes men will get women that weren't told they were cute or anything nice and treat them any kind of way because they know they aren't going anywhere. I don't want my child to be abused like that." I sat there thinking I wished my mother had protected me this way. Admittedly, I never got used to hearing her compliment her child. My insides turned, flipped and flopped when she did. In fact, I was embarrassed, angry, hurt and shamed all at the same time when she made that statement to her daughter.

It wasn't just her, but if anyone said anything positive about themselves, I thought they were boasting. If anyone said nice things about me, I didn't believe them. I felt they were lying or mocking me. Even if God gave me a compliment I threw Him in with the rest of huemanity. In my perspective He was no different to me than them. The problem was I couldn't see what other people saw in me. I never could. I didn't want to see me for fear they may just be right. And I would have to take responsibility for who I authentically was.

I was used to the feelings of unworthiness, self-pity, self-rejection, anger and blame. They were comfortable like old shoes and clothes and I didn't want to get rid of them at first, but my Creator said, "NO!" He told all of Hell's demons, "NO!" Why? Because my Soul cried out to my Creator to see and know the authentic me and my Creator responded to my sincere plea.

Last unmasking, I promise. This exercise comes from a friend that at her women's retreat wanted the women to do this at home and I ask you to do the same. She tweaked it for us at the retreat. We kept our clothes on. LOL! But we did have to write what we liked about ourselves.

Get a full length mirror, take off all of your clothes and look at yourself. Every stretch mark, dry skin, sagging or upright breast, stomach that may not be as flat as you would like it to be, lines or bags under your eyes, batwing arms, not so tight behind. Touch all those parts and tell them thank you!

Some of those people who shamed you are not alive anymore, but you are! They didn't have the courage or strength to stay the course, but you did! It was rough, challenging, hurtful, disappointing and unfair, but you stayed in the race. And your fearful and wonderful body didn't betray you with death. Yes, I know it doesn't move the way it used to. It was hit by a heart attack or stroke, cancer, sciatica, eczema, high blood pressure and now you are on insulin and taking pills but you are still here. Those battle scars couldn't stop you; you're resilient and worthy to be treated with respect and honor. And the first person to bestow that honor is you. Hug yourself until the tears flow hot and heavy against your face. Then write on a piece of paper what each part of your body has done for you. This is my list.

I thank you size seven and a half feet for carrying my two hundred and forty-two pound physical and emotional body these fifty odd years. You still look good in a pump and opened toe sandal. I thank you strong and flexible legs for walking, jumping, stretching and bending. When I put an anklet on you, you make the anklet look even better!

Thighs, what can I say about my large thighs. When I fell and hit the ground, you, and my behind worked in sync to keep my bones from breaking… LOL!

Stomach you may not be as flat as I would like you to be but you have prayed for others and birthed their dreams, concerns, and hopes into a reality for them. I humbly say thank you.

Breasts, you've never stood upright on your own, but you've held people and their tears, thank you.

131

Arms, with your bat wings you've embraced others, even when it hurt to the touch, but those times didn't let me think about my insecurities. You just opened up and welcomed them in.

Hands, you've written and typed a many a story down through the years. You've held so many things at one time to the point of hurting and aching and still you've never failed me when I needed you. I truly thank you!

Face, still youthful, the little girl I see in the pictures in my album. Thank you.

Skin, I thank you most of all because you took the brunt of everything. From every generational curse of rejection, no matter the Keloids or sagging of certain parts of the skin. I still see some of the prettiest, smoothest and softest skin ever. I love your toffee, mocha color with red undertones. I thank you Heavenly Father for thinking of me into existence.

I need to revisit my behind for a moment. You were called names and I hid you with clothing, so people, I thought wouldn't see you. I wore a trench coat in ninety degree weather and fainted on one of the busiest streets in downtown Gary. And now I repent for those times and ask you to forgive me. I have since learned that in other countries I would be considered beautiful and curvaceous. It's funny in our society today people are paying through the nose to have the natural curves that I was blessed with by God. Thank you for letting me know that when my husband comes, he will lay his head gently on you and he and I will know all is well with us.

Thank you "body" for you are "fearfully and wonderfully made," Psalms 139:14 (King James Version).

Now look at yourself and write your body a thank you note here in this space.

_____

_____
_____

Your Memories of
Pictures, Snapshots, or
Fragments
(Write, Draw, Doodle,
Color, Scribble)

18

The Trunk

Carbohydrates, proteins, dairy, sweets, all became my enemies. Anything I ate made me fat. At least that is what I was told. It was so confusing, that I didn't know what to eat and I was afraid to put anything in my mouth. It became painful to eat. I was afraid of food. Choosing what would or wouldn't make me fat, I figured I couldn't go wrong with a salad and water.

For breakfast, I had what my Mama prepared which was oatmeal, grits or cold cereal. Lunch was two Wonder bread, pimento loaf, American cheese, Hellmann's mayonnaise (lots of it) sandwiches, Jay's potato chips and Archway almond windmill cookies. Dinner on any night was chicken, pork chops, hamburger, or meatloaf; a vegetable could have been brussel sprouts, cabbage, broccoli, potatoes, string beans, cauliflower, peas or a vegetable medley. We had a garden in the back yard. Dessert was a holiday treat. That's not to say we didn't have sweets in the house, but cakes, pies, anything major like that was reserved for the holidays.

Me and Mama's bedroom was on the first floor, which was easy access to the kitchen. In our room was a trunk that was given to her in 1914 when she was nine years old. That trunk made the trek from Sheffield, Alabama to Gary, Indiana. The "Great Black Migration" from the south to the north, the land of opportunity to work in the thriving steel mills. That trunk is with me until this very day.

It held hopes, dreams, prayers, Black history books, church and personal finances, perfume, and midnight snacks. We waited until those whose bedrooms were upstairs retired and the house was dark. She would get up and I followed her to the kitchen. The only lights that were on were the nightlights in the dining room. The next light that came on was the one in the refrigerator. Down in the bin was the real sharp cheddar cheese; I mean the one with the bite to it that you felt in the back of your mouth when you bit into it. Earlier that day she fixed a tuna salad and I grabbed some bowls for her to fill them. The last thing she did was fill her plastic grayish white cup with ice and cold water (in which my sister has that cup to this day). We snuck back to our room and cut the night lamp on. She pulled the handkerchief out from under her pillow that her keys were attached to, opened her trunk and took out the Saltine crackers. Since our beds were pulled together to make one bed, I sat like Buddha on mine facing her and she sat with her back on the headboard and our feast was between us. We kept our voices down so no one would hear us upstairs.

A block of cheddar cheese, tuna and crackers is still my comfort food. It was our secret. It was my nourishment and one of the things that I felt good about eating. I ate it without guilt and shame because my Mama and I shared not only time, but it was her way of telling me she loved me. There were no rules or restrictions on what I couldn't eat, no name calling. I was free to eat in peace and love.

Those secrets in the dark trunk became a way of life for me. There was a public and a private way I ate. In public I ate salads so people wouldn't look at me like a spectacle in a sideshow circus. At home and at church I was under a microscope when I ate. The constant 'don't eat that or it will make you fat' remarks got on my everlasting nerve. So with *Guilt and Shame* I ate in private foods that contained fat, sugar and salt. *Fantasy* convinced me that everyone was looking at me and not just when I was eating. But deep down I wanted to be looked at, and not because of eating or being fat. I wanted people to see me and honestly just like me without verbally bashing me.

SIDE BAR: What I've discovered about perceptions of body image is if you're fat, skinny, tall, whatever, if your esteem has been wounded people may or may not notice you at all. Wounded souls may behave in several unauthentic ways (and these are just a few) to barge entry into gaining the attention of the people around them. Some people are silent, sullen or foreboding. This was my mode of operation for attention. Others are loud, condescending, obnoxious and rude. That is their way of demanding that they be recognized and force attention like a bratty two-year old. Both behaviors are unacceptable. And it all stems from *Rejection* of the authentic self. FINISHED.

People who barely knew me didn't judge me because I was fat. I learned to *judge* me and others because I'd been judged. I learned to be *self-righteous* to protect my heart and I projected that judging spirit on to others. I'd been hurt enough. I hid in the trunk beside the food, perfume, Black history books, finances, hopes and dreams.

MASK/Behaviors: Shame, Embarrassment, Self-Rejection, Self-Hatred, Judgmental, Self-Righteous, Spirit of Perfection, Critical of others

UNMASK: *Body Image Distortion, Bulimia, Anorexia and Obesity in children are being reported in the African American community in rising numbers among our children. The nature of the beast is the same low self-esteem issues, demeaning words spoken consistently until the true nature of a person goes into hiding.*

Don't let this be you! If you were shamed as a child about anything, do you really want to put your child through the same pain? You didn't deserve what they said and did to you, but your child doesn't deserve the same treatment either. They are not your past abusers, they are your children. Don't shame them. If you don't know how to talk to them seek help. Just ask the Divine and the help will come that is if you want it.

Segue Way

Into

Invisibility

Back Down Memory Lane
(Riperton Rudolph St. Lewis)
http://www. lyricstime.com

I stumbled on this photograph
It kinda made me laugh
It took me way back
Back down memory lane

I see the happiness. . . I see the pain
Where am I. . . back down memory lane

I see us standing there
Such a happy happy pair
Love beyond compare
look-a-there look-a-there

The way you held me. . . no one could tell me
That love would die. . . why oh why
Did I have to find this photograph
Thought I had forgot the past
But now I'm slippin' fast
Back down memory lane

I feel the happiness. . . I feel the pain
Here am I. . . back down memory lane
I'm in the sunshine. . . I'm in the rain

I don't wanna go traveling down
Faster than the speed of sound
Back down memory lane
Be still my foolish heart
Don't let this feelin' start
Back down memory lane
I don't wanna go. . . save me save me

141

This was the last Christmas that we were really a family. I was ten years old. This was the Christmas my siblings and I remember as being the best we've ever had. But it was also the year I emotionally left my family. Almost everything in this picture was a revelation that prophetically spoke what my life had been and was to come. The games I am leaning on are "Staying Alive" and "Séance." Behind me, but in the picture it appears they are sitting on top of my head, were my encyclopedias, and the stereo represented how music would play a very important part of my relationship with God and the manger (that we still have to this day) represented later in life Jesus' relationship to me. Hmm.

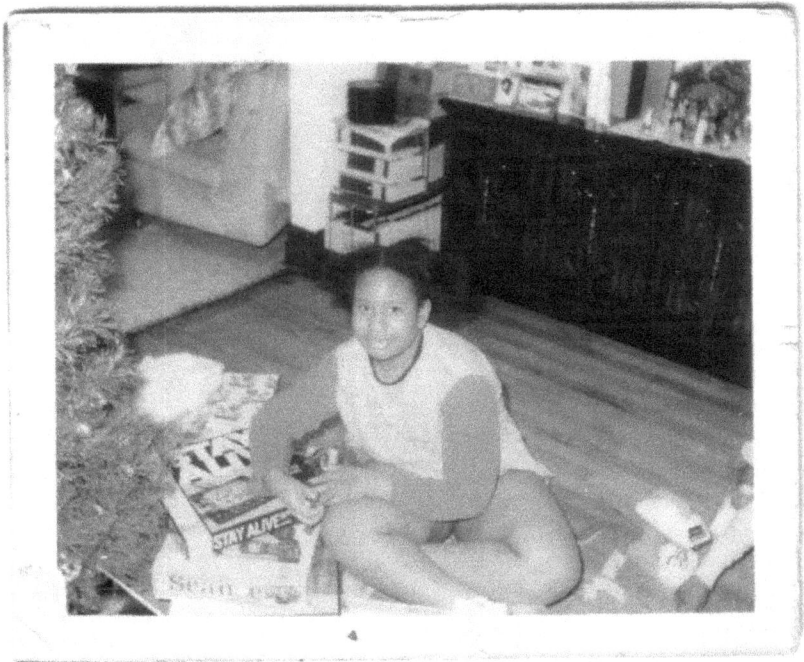

Your Memories of
Pictures, Snapshots, or
Fragments
(Write, Draw, Doodle,
Color, Scribble)

19

She Hated Me!

She hated me! From the first day to the last day of my fifth grade year in her class she didn't miss an opportunity to slight my weight or cause division between me and the kids she liked. The teachers, politicians, preachers, pretty, handsome or extremely smart kids, these were her pets.

My generation was the first of bussed kids, which produced latch-key kids. She called us a "bad element" in her school. She didn't even give us a chance. Now mind you this school sat in front of one of the oldest and worse projects in the city. I have nothing against the projects because eventually my family had to move in those same projects. But that story is for another book.

The second day of school, I was sitting in my seat and she told me "I was uncomfortable." I told her "I was fine." She turned around and through Kool Filter Kings (teacher's then could smoke on the premises), brown, gritting teeth told me I was uncomfortable and she was going to change my seat. My whole body shrunk down in the back of my desk. I felt ashamed once more of my body. She made another large young man go and get me a bigger desk from another classroom and put it in the middle of her classroom. It was only the second day of school and I stood in the middle of the classroom regretting the day I was born. Tears were sitting on the verge of my eyelids and I commanded them back down my ducts. My eyes stayed glued to the floor. I gathered my things and sat in my new place of *Shame*. She walked around me like a buzzard eyeing its prey and snidely said, "I'm doing this for your own good." If it was for my good, then why did I have this terrible, putrid feeling in the pit of my stomach? And I knew at that moment it was not going to get any better that year.

I thought the fighting would have at least stopped, but my reputation followed me to this school as well. I even tried to change my image by acting like the kids Mrs. Cameron liked, I failed. I ran around to the different cliques in school and nowhere did I fit in. I looked like a chicken with its head cut off. So I decided I wouldn't try to fit in anymore, just wherever they let me in I stayed until they didn't want me or I got bored. I pretended everyone liked me, but I knew only a few classmates did. In my mind, I fabricated this elaborate drama of being liked because when I was alone, I knew the real story and it hurt to my very core.

I loved to read and write. In Mrs. Roger's class at Douglass school, she inspired me to do so. Any magazine, book, pamphlet that was in the house I read it. We were given an assignment which required us to go to the library. We needed encyclopedias, but each time we went they were being used or pages were torn out of them. My mother was tired of going to the library after work. She bought me a set of encyclopedias. I was so happy. Regina and I used those encyclopedias for our assignment and received high marks.

During the holiday season, I read how Christmas was celebrated in certain African countries. I wrote a report and wanted to share it with the class. When I entered the classroom I put my books on my desk and walked to her desk. She looked over her thick, harshly gray rimmed glasses as if I was intruding upon her peaceful space. I proceeded through her unwelcome demeanor. I told her about the report and asked could I read it to the glass. Smugly without missing a beat, she said aren't you the little attention getter. Admittedly, I was an attention getter but not this time. I really wanted to share this information. Information was my avenue to view how the rest of the world lived and hopefully I would see for myself one day instead of reading about it.

I fought so much that year for her to notice my enthusiasm for learning, but it only brought her mocking words, evil glances, and laughter from classmates who were scared of her too and didn't want her to talk about them.

There was a class joker whose mother worked at the school. She was a beautiful woman inside and out. His mother often came to the class just to check on him because she knew her son. But this particular day she was desperately commanded by her son to come to our classroom.

Mrs. Cameron's form of punishment was to take her huge man broad, flat fingers with eagle sharp nails and peck you at the very top of your head real hard. This one time in class I appreciated the joker for telling his mother about Mrs. Cameron. He began to cry after she pecked him on his head. She told him that since he acted like a baby he needed to go and suck his Mama's titty. That boy ran so fast out the classroom to get his mother, I didn't even see the door open. His mother had a high pitched voice like a canary and that day she flew up the stairs. Her face red and chest heaving, she entered the classroom and politely told Mrs. Cameron to come out in the hallway. The whole class was rooting for the joker's mother that day, even the kids she liked smiled. That day the joker's mother railed into her behind and the whole classroom breathed, literally, breathed. You could feel the atmosphere become lighter. Someone fought for us who had the voice of a canary, but that day her eagle came out and avenged not just her son but the entire class.

I told my family how she treated me periodically throughout the year, but I grew up in the "old school" mentality that those in authority were right and I was to stay in a child's place. I suffered that year with an atrocious teacher. She was more interested in breaking your will and pressuring you to become what she thought you should be. Individualism and uniqueness were seen as rebellious and that was unacceptable. I needed a break and I did get one, my art teacher Ms. Graves.

She was stout, light skin, wore a huge Afro, colorful dashikis and hard black round framed glasses. And she was the bomb! Her style of teaching was easy, relaxed and fun. Learning the history of art in different cultures, sculptures, coloring, paintings, and how to mix colors to get another color was cool. But what I discovered that year filled me with pure joy. I discovered that I could draw Disney characters free handed. I showed Ms. Graves and she was shocked. At first she thought I traced the characters until I showed her in class. She told me to keep drawing and don't stop. I breathed naturally when I sat and drew pictures because for the most part I held my breath out of fear and stress the rest of the time. I was really good at art though. I saw my own talent and skill. No one had to approve of it or affirm me. I saw it for myself.

MASK/Behaviors: Self-Hatred, Shame, Embarrassment, Hatred for those in authority, Fear of Authority, Conformist, Fiercely Independent

UNMASK: This was the first year of bussed kids to schools out of the area I lived in. I hated my new school as teacher Mrs. Cameron. This woman, from the very first day of school, verbally and physically abused not just me, but any child that was not included in her parameters of who she liked. Her disdain for uniqueness was seen as rebellion. Her words, facial expressions and body movements spoke volumes and were used to discourage any gift or talent a child wanted to share with the class. If it were not for my art teacher Ms. Graves, I don't think I would have made it through my first year at this new school. Even though I didn't need Ms. Grave's affirmation of my drawing it was extremely comforting just to hear her words and sit in her space. They were my emotional life raft to keep me afloat.

On the other hand, my parent, and family, when I would tell them about Mrs. Cameron's treatment of not just me, but the other kids they always sided with her or any adult for that matter. I knew then to tell them of an adult mistreating me would not garner any support from them. I was on my own to try and defend myself or more so retreat into Fantasy's lair where I was appreciated and heard.

Those in authority are not always right nor are your children for that matter. There is an adage that states, "There is your side, the other side and truth." But I believe strongly it is up to you to thoroughly investigate ALL sides involved before making a rash decision. Look under the surface to see and hear what really happened and LISTEN to your child. OPEN your eyes and really see INTO your child. Go beyond what happened to you as a child so you won't make the same mistake that was made with you. Your child will greatly appreciate it if they see you approaching their teacher or whoever is in authority to battle for them. Seeing you take up for them says so much more than lip service or doing nothing at all. They need to know you, their parent/guardian is on their side. Even if they had a negative part in what happened showing up lets them know you care about their feelings, their thoughts, their words. I, on the other hand, knew I was on my own.

Your Memories of
Pictures, Snapshots, or
Fragments
(Write, Draw, Doodle,
Color, Scribble)

20

But I'm A Student Council Representative!

I played hard that day in gym class. Volleyball was my favorite sport. My gym teacher Mrs. Golden called me "one hand Sally." After gym, I went to the locker room to wash and dress for my next class. There was a girl in my class, I will call her Bailey, and she loved the feel of a girl's breast. We had to fight her off, but a part of me liked her touch. I kept this to myself because it was the same feeling as back in second grade, or, when I fantasized about guys that didn't like me or the guys I thought were cute. I filed this correlation in the back of my mind.

We left the gym and went back to Mrs. Cameron's class where she announced a student council meeting the next day. Earlier that month I'd been nominated as a student council representative for my class. Each class elected a student as a representative to address the concerns of their entire class and also suggested fund raisers to pay for activities. I was so excited when she told us about the meeting. I went home that day from school to prepare for the meeting and dig my feet in to participate. I was used to being a part of committees. At church I was involved in various groups and working with others for a common goal. This was when I enjoyed it before it became an obligatory task.

I finished my homework, ate dinner and went upstairs to take a bath. This was a part of my alone time. I locked the door, turned the water on, leaned my head back and listened to the water's song. An urgent knock on the door jarred my serenade.

"Lana, open the door and let me in. I have to use the bathroom."

It was my mother. I wished she had gone downstairs to use the bathroom, but I knew that was not happening.

"I'm taking a bath, Mama."

"Girl, if you don't open this door, I know what your body looks like. I had you."

I got up and opened the door. My sanctity had been defiled. My peace of mind was trumped to her urgent bladder release. I sat back down in the tub and tried to regain some territory. But it only got worse. My mother screamed.

"What's that in your draws?"

I looked at my panties and I promise you I didn't see what she was talking about.

"What are you talking about?"

"That!" She pointed again to my panties. She picked them up and shoved them an inch from my face. I moved back because they smelled like fish. I did see a spot of blood, but it didn't register what she thought it was. I asked her if she was talking about the blood. She nodded her head in the affirmative. I told her maybe I fell playing volleyball and hurt myself.

"Get out of the tub - NOW!" She screamed like *Death* was here and I was leaving with him.

I got out of the tub and realized I hadn't washed. I told her so. She told me to stand up and bathe. I asked why? She stated because I told you so. I've always hated that answer because it's not an answer. That is an adult way to avoid answering the question when they don't want to answer the question or they don't know the answer. I washed, got out of the tub and went about my normal routine. I didn't know what to expect, but it couldn't be good after my mother's scream.

No one said anything to me as I walked out the bathroom. I walked down the stairs to my room where my Mama, my protector, who I knew would answer my questions. The last step of the landing I looked at the dark living room, dining room and kitchen. The only light on was in my bedroom. I walked in our room and my Mama was sitting at the foot of the bed near the trunk. I sat in her rocking chair. She said nothing, not a word. I decided to break the tension.

"Mama, what is going on? And why did she scream like a crazy woman when she saw blood in my panties?"
"She will explain it to you. But you are now a woman, no longer a little girl. Your mother will tell you the rest."
As I looked back on this moment Mama reminded me of the Oracle in *The Matrix* and I was *Neo*. The only thing missing was baking cookies and the little boy was not showing me how to become one with the spoon. And all I wanted was answers from anybody.

I walked back upstairs. When I got to the top tier my mother's room was dark except for the desk lamp and the tip of her Kool cigarette glowing as she blew smoke into the semi-darkness. I sat down at her metal desk waiting for what I didn't know. She blew smoke again and again and I was getting tired of this forty's bar room scene. I had a student council meeting the next day.

"So what is going on Mama?"

"Well." She took another long drag when I asked her that question.

"That blood, well, I mean, Lana your body is changing and..." I was getting so tired of her beating around the bush.

"Am I going to die?" I was tired of this spooky session.

"No."

"Well, if I'm not going to die what is the blood about?"

"I'm trying to explain, Lana. Your body is now a woman's body and you can have babies."

"Babies!" I screamed.

"Yes, babies. Your body is going to pass blood once a month and you will have to wear pads." She picked up a tampon. I had seen them before in her room, but didn't think anything of it.

"I'm going to have to wear that?"

"No, not this, this goes inside your tunecy, which is called a vagina. We just say that word so it doesn't sound so vulgar."

Finally, I found out what it was really called and it didn't sound vulgar to me.

"You will wear a pad that is flat and looks like a lot of cotton balls wrapped in special netting. You will wear this between your legs for several days to catch the blood. Since I don't wear them, I will buy some tomorrow because the stores are closed now."

That sounded vulgar to me.

"You mean I will have to miss school tomorrow?"

"Yes."

"I can't. I have a student council meeting tomorrow and I'm the representative for my class."

"Well, you are going to miss it tomorrow. I will call your teacher and let her know why."

"I hate this. What is this called?"

"It's called menstruation, bloody Mary, or period as adults call it."

"Why?"

"Aside from the first formal name the other two are just names passed down from generation to generation to describe when it occurs. It is bloody, and it is for a period of time, and the period looks like a spot, and that is what the blood looks like, a conglomerate of spots. What's wrong?"

"I'm mad because I'm going to miss my first student council meeting and I'm the representative."

"Good night Lana." And that was it.

I walked back downstairs scared, mad and a part of me still felt like I was going to die. I walked to my room, looked at my Mama's sad face. She looked like this was a moment she'd dreaded but had no control over because it's a natural process.

The next day I moped around all morning wondering how the meeting went and what did these pads look like my mother was going to bring home. She came home at lunch time with this brown paper bag. My mother, Mama and aunt convened in my Mama's room surrounding this bag of pads like an initiation process.

155

My mother pulled out this contraption that looked like a guillotine. It had steel hooks and long pieces of elastic where the pad would be attached to. The pad was so long. I knew once I put it on, everyone would see it. They looked at my face and laughed because I was determined to find a way around wearing this guillotine and this pad the size of an elephant. It was funny out of this whole farce my mind was only on one thing. I vowed never to miss another student council meeting. Screw a period.

🎭   *MASK/Behaviors: Feeling important, Martyr (neglecting self for others), Non-Celebratory Spirit of Femininity*

UNMASK: Being elected as a representative made me feel important. Missing that meeting was more important than understanding I was at an important juncture in my life. But it was not presented to me in that fashion, nor was it to my mother, or her mother or her mother before her. It was looked upon as the gateway to pregnancy. So pregnancy was seen as something to be feared and not as a moment of joy. Why? Most pregnancies in my family were conceived from wounded souls. They either saw it as a religious act, to replenish the earth, or, just got caught. Generations of teachings that were taught in fear and ignorance sullied the two most wonderful rites of passages. I wish the women in my family could have sat with me on the night I watched these rites of passage celebrated on a television show.

On the "Cosby Show" in season seven, episode nine, Claire took Rudi out of school the day she started her menstruation. She called it "Woman's Day." She unraveled the mystery surrounding this moment and revealed the most loving aspects of the joy of being a female, a woman. I cried that day. Femininity and children were shunned in my family because of how it had been presented in a man-made doctrine of Religion and Shame.

I've neglected my body since I can remember. Self-hatred and loathing of my body down through the years has taken its toll on my body and mind. I'm just now beginning to appreciate the wonder of my body be it not what the media idolizes or sometimes I wish I had but it has proven its endurance through the challenges I might not have made it through.

We must be vigilant in sharing information with our girls in a manner that celebrates them as females. It is a joy to be a female. From the beginning of their menstrual to marriage to childbirth, they need to understand and see couples who desire a child, planning for a child, single women who want a career, to educate themselves, be entrepreneurs, and desire marriage with a partner who welcomes children and values females. Maybe, just maybe low self-esteem that leads to teen pregnancy, venereal diseases, anorexia, bulimia, obesity, and suicide will decrease in our girls. I pray the elder women are healed, so they can share their story with the girls. This will greatly assist in each female newborn arriving into a family and society of healing and unafraid females who love being a female so they can be taught self-love from the onset.

Your Memories of
Pictures, Snapshots, or
Fragments
(Write, Draw, Doodle,
Color, Scribble)

21

Crown and Glory

Who cut your hair? I sat there wondering what she was talking about. *I'm going to ask you again. Who cut your hair?* I didn't know what she was talking about. Really, I didn't! She called in my mother and Mama to look at my hair to see where it was supposedly cut. They asked me question after question of who cut my hair and I told them no one had cut my hair.

They blamed Regina for cutting my hair and I defended her like Perry Mason. It was funny they blamed her for cutting my hair, when every chance they got they compared me to her. The tirade my relatives were going off on confused me to use her in that light, in fact, it was downright comical. I knew I could lie my tail off, but I did it when it convenience me to look larger than life or hide something I actually did. As much as I disliked being compared to her, I knew this was wrong. *I'm not going to ask you again. Who cut your hair?* And again, I tell them no one has touched my hair. They start reminiscing about how I was born with no hair and how long it took them to grow it. Personally, I didn't care. I was still in shock of how they deduced that due to my hair being longer than Regina's she cut my hair. I kept thinking, of course, to myself, how stupid. They even approached her mother with this accusation. I was so embarrassed. This incident put a slight riff in our relationship. I felt bad because she and no one else touched

159

my hair. They didn't think about the relaxer they'd put in my hair because they were tired of those Saturday night hot comb pressing rituals.

The relaxer was to put an end to scorched ears because I wasn't holding them down, burning my edges because I moved when I should have been still and when the comb fell down my back, oh, couldn't blame me for that, they were tired. I'm not saying sometimes it wasn't true. Every child moves when they sit for so long, but not every time it occurred was it my fault. So to put an end to those rituals and blaming sessions, the relaxer was the answer. But no one thought about that decision. It was easier to blame than accept the responsibility for a joint decision that was eating my hair.

There was a relaxer back in the seventies called Ultra Sheen. There were two types of relaxer, one was for mild and the other was super. I can't remember which one they used, but they both were powerful for virgin hair at my age. People on the block knew when someone was relaxing hair because it could be smelled outside. Once my uncle took a bath and was looking for the tub cleanser. The relaxer was sitting in the corner of the tub without the label, it had come off. He thought it was a cleanser and cleaned the bathtub with it. That tub sparkled for several days in spite of how many baths were taken in it. And they put that stuff on my hair in which it did take my hair out. They couldn't blame that one on me. So what were they to do now? What do you think had to be done? Yep, cut it. Let the rest of the relaxer grow out and back to the Saturday night ritual of the hot comb and pressing my hair.

They called our cousin who was a beautician (and I believed a witch as well) to assist in growing it back. The weekend ritual was now Friday night Glover's Mange, and Saturday was mid-morning washing, conditioning and sitting under the bonnet hair dryer. This was followed by greasing of my scalp with Sulfur 8, Bergamot oil or Blue Magic and finally, the pressing of the hair with the hot comb on the oven or ceramic stove. This was my regiment for several months until my hair grew back.

After this debacle, I knew if I just agreed with whatever I was being blamed for the screaming, hollering and arguing would cease. Pushing my true feelings down was becoming much easier. I stopped trying to defend myself because no matter what I said my opponent proved me wrong. From this point on I learned I didn't know how to defend myself. But I did learn how to put ALL the blame on me just to squash arguing and the screaming voices. I was the embodiment of *Blame*. I swallowed, gulped, shoved down my feelings and words somewhere inside of me until I stopped thinking and feeling anything and about anyone. What was a normal feeling to an emotionally healthy person was not normal to me. I felt *wrong* all the time. I was the embodiment of *Wrong*. I greatly feared people. I was confused about what and how I should feel, and being *Wrong* became a way of life. I learned to choose my battles, but the war was forthcoming and my stamina was at ninety-nine point eight percent gone.

MASK/Behaviors: Passive/aggressive,   Avoid Conflict, Loner, Embodiment of Blame and Wrong, Confused about what I authentically felt, Emotional Dishonesty, Scared and refused to express my true feelings, Denial of Anger, and a Perverted Fear of man

UNMASK: Listen to your children tell their side of the story. Research the situation first before you accuse them. But first you must know your child and that means paying attention to them.

My family thought they knew me, but they didn't. The real me was fading to black in that I didn't know the real me from the mask. All I knew is I wanted the yelling and blaming to stop and for people to leave me alone. I spent more time by myself, talked to myself and answered back. Being alone kept me from being noticed, ridiculed and blamed; it kept me away from those who loved me?

Please listen to your children and don't do to them what they did to you as a child. My relatives heard what they wanted to hear to feel right about a situation. It had nothing to do with the present moment. It was the past, they were remembering and fighting. I got caught in the crossfire of their wounded childhood memories and the present moment.

22

Being Me, Can't Be

It's the middle of the school year and the fight in me waned hard to stay alive at home, church and school. I couldn't get any relief anywhere except under the basement stairs where it was dark, quiet and with *Fantasy*. I could think in the darkness. It was my place of solitude and peace, like Superman's lair. It was the only place I felt powerful. I could hear my thoughts instead of a cruel word about eating too much, being fat, screaming at me or blaming me for something. Did they ever think of their actions or take responsibility for their part in any of the situations? No. They didn't. I was always in a catch twenty-two. I was damned if I do and damned if I don't.

Even attending church on a regular was becoming painful. I could count on someone mentioning my weight. Be ye young or an adult it didn't matter. The words hurled out of their mouths as if I had no feelings at all. And because I was taught not to speak back to elders, I took the hits with a conciliatory smile or a nod of my head. My rock, my protector Mama couldn't even block some of the hits, especially at home. I tried to do what she said and pray, but I knew God had turned his back on me too. I realized that my prayers didn't change things. I felt like Mama and God lied to me and little did I know it was about to get worse. Another person was coming to live in **my** home.

163

I had to share **our** bedroom, bed, and protector, **my** Mama. I didn't want to share my Mama. She still was the only one who cared about me. No, she was not overly affectionate but it was in the way she did things for me that I knew she loved me. And I was not ready to share the only person that was on my side.

The new relative walked in the house all smiles and hugs. I pretended to go along with the charade. Remember, I could act extremely well too. No, I didn't know she was just as scared as I was and probably afraid she wouldn't be accepted by a family she hardly knew, nor did I care. I had already lost ground with family, teachers, peers and certain people at church. I was almost ten years old and I already knew that I would never have a boyfriend, husband or a child. I would be alone. I needed my Mama, **my** Mama. I needed her presence and belief because mine wasn't good enough for God.

Everyone loved my new relative including my Mama. I was losing my Mama. I could see it in her eyes. I understood why they all loved her because she was short of being Wonder Woman and all I had was an excellent memory. She could corn roll, press and style hair. Hazel, the maid on television, consulted with her to cook, clean a house, wash and iron clothes. I on the other hand was officially named by my John Wayne uncle, whom I adored, the *fat, lazy, trifling* child. My family never thought once about what they hadn't taught me. When I came home from school my Mama had cooked and cleaned the house. I was forbidden to touch the Sears & Roebuck washer and dryer because I was told I would break it, but I was never taught how to use it. I was the *fat, lazy, trifling* one where those words came out of their mouths swifter than the wind.

Even Regina my next door neighbor betrayed me. The new relative taught us this game called *Ace Boom Coon*. It is a game where you have a composition book filled with questions for your friends to respond to. It was our way of knowing if our friends liked us in return, what they liked to do, or not to do, if they had a boyfriend, etc. We would run to each other's house and put these letters or composition books in our mailboxes.

My letters as my new relative were kept in separate shoe boxes underneath my, excuse me, I stand corrected, our bed. One weekend my relative spent it with her mother and I was lying down on the floor between the bed, wall and closet. I saw the boxes underneath the bed and I knew it was wrong, but I stuck my hand in her box and randomly pulled out a letter. I read it and wished to God I had not. It stated *I like you better than Lana. She likes to play in the dirt and you like to do girl things. I want you to be my friend instead of Lana.* Those words further solidified that I was not good enough to be a friend with females. I believed that with everything in me. I was contaminated.

Anything that defined being a female I rejected. My interpretation of female meant the color pink, of course, playing with dolls, and girls couldn't be my friend. I would only allow boys to be my friends. And I was a boy since the girls didn't get dirty. I asked the question of God or to any Being that hopefully was listening to me. *Why was I born? I don't look like a girl. I mean I have breasts and a tunecy, no, I have a vagina like girls but they don't look like me, or like to play with*

165

me or like me. I told this God I was short, fat, light brown skin with acne and a keloid on my left ear. Other girls were tall, beautiful skin, long hair and small. I cried until I couldn't cry anymore. I vowed that any male that wanted to be my friend would be my best friend forever. I didn't need females as friends.

I stayed on that floor it seemed like ages. All I knew was when I got up I was a different person on the inside. When the new relative returned from her weekend away, I knew she and Regina would be hanging together so I retreated to my place of solitude to be with *Fantasy*. She welcomed me with open arms to tell me how beautiful I was, how the boys were going to love me, and I didn't need girlfriends. I only needed her and the fantasies she and I created together.

MASK/Behaviors: Self-Rejection, Mild Schizophrenia, Self-Hatred, Jealousy, Rejection of Femininity, Abandonment, Anger, Rage, Silent, Loner, Pride, Unworthiness, Spirit of Perfection

UNMASK: A child should always know that their parent(s) or guardians love them. When love between you and your child has been firmly established in the foundation of their early life, no matter whom, another child or their friend, your child knows beyond a shadow of a doubt they are number one in your eyes. I can't stress enough that in your child's earlier years teaching them to share goes beyond things but also applies to people. You have to make them a part of the process with you. If you work with youth groups or neighborhood kids allow your child to be a part of that sect. Talk to them about what you do and why you do it. If not, someone else will embrace them and lead them to activities or other groups that will show them love and it may not be the kind they hoped for, but love is love, right?

Teach them how to clean, cook, do hair, etc., don't assume they know just by watching you. Make them a part of the process so they can become comfortable in basic housekeeping regiments. This is vital to their growth. They won't always live at home.

Don't assume they know you love them because you are there with them or you buy them things. It's how you present your love to them that will define love to them. If it's presented in an abusive manner, then abuse they will associate with love. If it's a distant relationship, then more than likely they will love people, including themselves from a distance. I became a loner because I felt I wasn't good enough for anyone to love, so I didn't know what love looked like. I was unlovable. Don't let this become your child. Go back in your childhood and see the pattern. If you have perpetuated the pattern to your child, then seek to find a way to break it and learn an emotional healthy way to love. You must first learn to love yourself, then your child. Your child deserves to know they are loved and deserves to be loved so they can love themselves. And in turn, they will healthily love others who come into their lives.

In later years Regina and I talked over lunch about our lives where we were transparent with one another about our upbringing.

Your Memories of
Pictures, Snapshots, or
Fragments
(Write, Draw, Doodle,
Color, Scribble)

23

Goldblatt's Stockings

I was growing up and my legs were too chubby to wear socks plus it wasn't becoming of a young girl at least that is what I was told. I was also being made to wear a long line girdle because I jiggled. Clothes were a major issue due to cost and size. The bigger the person it required more material which inflated the cost. My clothes were not store bought cute anymore. They were becoming matronly, like muumuus. Stores like Lane Bryant I visited when money was plentiful. Kmart, Zayre's and a store in downtown Gary, I can't remember the name, were slowly but surely becoming the places I shopped. In two years, Lane Bryant would be a luxury that was visited once a year.

There was another store in Gary called Goldblatt's. It was a precursor to Wal-Mart. It had everything you wanted, but it had the feel of a boutique and select furniture. It carried all the perfumes you found in any Macy's store down to your daily deodorant. I remember down in the basement was the record shop. Any musical group that was out at that time whether R&B, Funk, Ballads, Gospel, Rock, Country, it didn't matter your forte Goldblatt's had your preference. From 33's to 45's to eight track tapes (in which I still have) you would find it there. They were one of the last stores that had courtesy people manning the elevator. I loved that store!

One Saturday afternoon, my relative and I went there to purchase stockings for church on Sunday. Now up until that point my stockings were purchased for me. But this time I wanted to see if I could do it myself. To be honest, I didn't know the criteria for buying stockings because when I looked up they were on my bed. I mimicked my relative looking for a particular color. I didn't know about the size. Yeah, I know it sounds stupid, but I thought if I looked for the color I wanted, the stockings would fit me. I bought them, took them home and showed them to my Mama. I was so proud of myself. She looked at the label and told me I had the wrong size. I told one of my adult relatives in the house of my incorrect purchase and asked her to drive me back to the store to exchange them. Immediately she started screaming at me saying how dumb I was to purchase the wrong size and why did I purchase them if I didn't know what to do. I was bewildered, confused, hurt and angry. Was there not anything I could do right?

Why did she have to scream at me like I was an animal? Couldn't she have just showed me what to look for and then I would have known how to purchase my own stockings? Her screaming at me made me cower and shiver on the inside. And this followed me well into my adult years before I learned that her bark was worse than her bite. I hated the very sound of her voice and all subsequent voices well into the future.

I learned to detect, control, aggressiveness, bully, anger and meanness in anyone's tone. When I heard it, I shivered, cowered, and my throat closed up. I was too afraid to speak up. This only enhanced the *People Pleasing, Non-Confrontational* wimp I was becoming minute by minute. The weight I was accumulating from wearing these masks overpowered my metabolism. I was wearing the weight of people I'd lost count of and the number was rising. I couldn't detect my core personality anymore.

I only saw the *fat, lazy and trifling* girl that was good at *Lying*. This was my survival tool to keep me away from the enemies that I lived with, associated with at church, and school. Fantasizing was my reality. I dreamt of another family coming to take me to live with them. I just knew my real family had a search warrant out for me and any day they would come to the front door and claim me as their child. I use to sit on the porch waiting for them to come and get me. I was more than ready to go. Even my Mama was not taking up for me like she used to, but little did I know her health was beginning to decline. She had not been diagnosed with Diabetes -yet.

This era was my beginning stages of thoughts of suicide. I wanted to die. If I was sent to earth to be a verbal punching bag for hurt people, then I no longer wanted to be a part of this earth. Death was an option I could live with until I asked my Mama about killing yourself and she said you'd go to hell for doing that. Still, I never threw the option out. I just put it to the side until I could think about it and later to try and talk God into making an exception.

I conceded more to the powers that be at home, school and church. Every place was like the haunted house to me. I didn't know when a spook would come out to scare me. I learned to walk lightly, speak softly, almost not audible. I stayed under the stairwell every chance I got. My mind was shutting down to my real thoughts and whatever someone

171

wanted me to think, that's what I thought. I became invisible in thought, word and deed. I became whatever the flavor of the moment needed me to be.

Chameleon, imitator of voices, thought and mannerism at this point, authenticity was ninety-nine percent gone. If I wasn't good enough to use a breath to teach me how to choose stockings, then I wasn't good enough to be seen or heard. My very breath was not good enough to speak from an honest, sincere place. I parroted what others wanted to hear which mainly were themselves. I, Lana was leaving the home, school, church, and life long before Elvis left.

🦎 *MASK/Behaviors: Non-Confrontational, Deaf & Dumb, Self-Hatred, Self-Rejection, Mild Schizophrenia, Rage, Angry, Conformist, Confused, Fear of people, Fear of trying new things, Fear of living, Murderer, Suicidal thoughts, Voice stripped*

UNMASK: I wanted to die, I wanted to run away; I wanted someone to take me away, anyone to take me away from this hell. Suicide never left my thoughts. It was always the running option that sounded so good. Why? Because it was permanent and I would have been at peace.

This is what happens to a child when it has reached this level. Columbine was the manifestation of what I thought of long before it happened. I murdered those who hurt me in my mind a thousand times over with unspeakable deaths. I didn't feel bad in the beginning when I started fantasizing about killing people. Not until my adult years sitting in church listening to my pastor talk about the Spirit of Murder. It was then I felt conviction and repented. But until that moment I did it to feel powerful and to get revenge because I felt helpless and trapped. I wanted to curse everyone out, scream at them how I felt, verbally and physically hurt them and snatch their esteem and voice, and call them out of their name, but I knew I wouldn't. No. I couldn't talk back for extreme fear of being hit, blamed or humiliated, so my venomous thoughts became my weapon of choice.

To add insult to injury I turned a deaf ear to my authentic voice and dumb to my authentic thoughts. I refused to give my honest opinion on anything because I couldn't verbally spar with people to defend my position. And most people that debated were cruel and enjoyed cutting the person down, rather than addressing the subject. I also felt that if anyone disagreed with what I was saying meant "I am wrong." And "I" was the embodiment of Wrong. I couldn't differentiate between my opinions being challenged and the other person attacking me. I personified Wrong like Rejection. I stopped talking. My voice and mind was Legion. I conformed to whomever I was with out of Fear of people.

Some days I would sit on my porch fantasizing about my real family coming to the door and picking me up. I would see a father, mother, and older siblings coming to get me and take me to our place out west, California, or east, New York. I created these scenes where they told the people I was living with they had been looking for me, and they paid them to release me so I could return with them. That is how bad I wanted to be away from my family, church, school and Gary, Indiana. In my mind anywhere was better than this space I existed in.

I ceased living to accommodate those around me while I sat underneath the stairwell and lived through Fantasy. And that is where I continued to live for years to come.

Your Memories of
Pictures, Snapshots, or
Fragments
(Write, Draw, Doodle,
Color, Scribble)

24

Those Damn Speeches

Certain things were expected when you have a Mama involved in almost every auxiliary group in church as well as the church secretary for over forty-five years. So here I was at church living in the light of her status and reputation. What was I to do? Urrr, you're right, get with the program. It just went with the territory.

Being the Sunday school superintendent every sacred holiday there was a 3:30 p.m. afternoon program. It was like clockwork, it was expected. I dreaded those times of the year. I knew I had to memorize a speech that was a soliloquy. I wanted a four line poem to memorize and be done with, but no, I was the superintendent's granddaughter. At Christmas my speech told the events that led up to the birth of Christ in rhyme and at Easter I told the events of Jesus' life, death, and resurrection. Shoot! I felt like Jesus carrying his cross every time a program was held.

I begged my Mama to please give me a shorter speech. At least narrow it down from a thirty-two stanza speech to sixteen. That was a fair trade I thought. She looked at me as if I had grown a tail and two horns. I accepted my punishment as I went to my corner downstairs in the basement to learn my epic.

Each day that led up to the 3:30 p.m. afternoon program my stomach and head hurt. Why did I have to be singled out? Why couldn't I be like everyone else? No. That was not good enough. I had to be put on display. Much as I loved my Mama around those times of the year, I wished she had left me alone or either granted me what I wanted. But being the trooper, nut, or just plain scared of losing her love during those times, I learned my lines and recited them to her nightly.

It's the Sunday of the 3:30 p.m. afternoon Christmas program. Everyone is excited because of the holiday and goody bags that will be given after the program. I just wanted the torture to be over. The Sunday school teachers gathered their classes to take them upstairs to the main sanctuary. I sat with my class on the left hand side of the church wishing the devotions could last just a little longer. In fact, why not sing "Silent Night" in the beginning of the program so the Holy Ghost could touch my Mama and she could shout for at least another fifteen minutes. But just like clockwork, she started on time and went by the program as typed.

The younger classes always went first to say their one liner and some didn't even get that far. They saw the crowd of people, and ended up crying and running back to their parents. I knew how they felt. I wished I could have ran out of the church and never looked back. The primary and junior classes went next, in which I was a part of. I dreaded it. My teacher always made me go last because either she wanted to be remembered for having the student who memorized a book, or, I just had the longest poem in the 3:30 p.m. afternoon Christmas program. Then she introduced me…"and now last but not least is little" I hated my name. No, literally, I hated my name.

I approached the front of the sanctuary wishing I was far away on a bus tour. I turned around to face the congregation, scanned for a second who was in the pews, and then looked over at my Mama sitting with the book in her hand of the poem I was to recite. I started watching their faces as I opened with the entrance of Mary's angelic visit and halfway through the journey I noticed a peer of mine eyes, but more importantly I noticed her middle finger propped on her nose. My ears stopped up, the five hundred seat sanctuary became extremely small, and the air was being sucked out of the room. All my attention was drawn to her finger as I stumbled over words and heard giggles. That giggle broke the spell and gave me a minute to divert my attention to my Mama but she never looked up from that book. I quickly finished the epic, rushed back to my seat as the adults clapped and my peers mockingly laughed. All I could think of was *why? Why did she hate me? All I wanted was to fit in and be her friend. What was wrong with me?* Never once did I think what was wrong with her and my peers.

I don't know if my Mama having me out in front was a curse or a blessing. She recognized early that I had an excellent memory and maybe she was training the leader in me. But the damage of *Rejection* had severely wounded my esteem and my vitals were shutting down in spite of her waning protection and feeble attempts to keep me in the forefront. I think a part of her knew about the *Rejection* history in our family. She knew the generational sins of the family because she knew the guilt she carried of things she'd fallen prey to. Sometimes I felt like a poster child where I had to be better, perform better, act better, do better, be the perfect child. When all I wanted was for them to love me, have friends, and to be me.

The person who lifted her bird finger during my speech gave me the most grief of all church peers. I never understood why she hated me so until I was an adult. I found out she was being compared to me in her home by her guardian so anytime she could embarrass me, lie on me, or shame me she did. She was a victim like I was but when you're a child you don't know that. I did forgive her when this was revealed to me. We both were products of wounded generational emotions. It's a shame because if we were valued, or more importantly, our families knew our value we possibly could have been friends.

🎭 *MASK/Behaviors: Perfection, Hypocrite, Fear of Man, Conformity, Deaf & Dumb spirit*

UNMASK: What once was a joy became such a drudgery of sorts. I liked memorizing speeches and performing in front of audiences as a young girl, but the older I got the more I dreaded it. I didn't like being seen by people. I wanted to be in the background away from the crowd, the mockery, and the jeers. I just wanted to be left alone. I liked the solitary, reclusive way I was becoming. It was safe, comfortable and peaceful. No one to compare, compete, scream, or belittle me. I was by myself and that was how I wanted it to remain. But I couldn't at church because my Mama was involved in almost every aspect or auxiliary in some sort of way. I was attached to her hip and that made me an accessory to my own verbal assassination. It was like I could never just be. Whether that be left alone or to just be me. I just wanted to be free. Was that a crime? No, it was a hueman right. But when you have hurt people hurting you, and an army of one trying her best to defend me, and at the same time using me to participate in what was a great part of her life, namely the church, I was losing ground. The real me was ninety-nine point nine percent gone. The mask I wore in front of the people in the church was a placating smile, but behind it, I cried as I participated in any capacity I was asked or told to do.

I understand that children have gifts that need to be nurtured but not to be used against them. Children will enjoy their gifts when they know they are loved for who they are, when they know they are protected, when they know that with or without the gift you just love them because they are hueman.

Your Memories of
Pictures, Snapshots, or
Fragments
(Write, Draw, Doodle,
Color, Scribble)

Purge #2 – Hannah's Daughter

Other: "I'm going to show you how to do the "pussy." My girlfriend showed me how to do it and I'm going to show you but you can't tell anyone."

Me: I won't tell anyone.

Other: You get on top of me and rub your pussy against mine real hard.

Narrator: Lana does and it feels good to her.

Other: My friend sucked my titty. You suck mine.

Me: Okay, I will.

Narrator: She sucks her breast and then a voice not visible in the room, but in her head tells her to go lower. She does. Her stomach, the top of her thighs and then the voice tells her to kiss "it." She does.

Other: Girl, what are you doing? My girlfriend didn't do this to me.

Narrator: She starts kissing her in the private place; the place called tunecy but Lana knows it now as vagina. This is the place blood flows once a month for several days to rid it of old blood. This is the process to purify and be cleansed. Lana goes deeper on invisible instruction to suck the small piece of meat. It reminds her of a small ding-a-ling. This is the name her family calls a penis. She does. Seeing how it pleases the other person she feels powerful and good at something. She finishes like a pro and she's only ten years old. She feels superior in this act. Finally, something she feels good about and powerful over another person. This person will need me for something now. She will respect me, like me and not shun me.

Other: We've got to do this again.

THE END

Was this wrong? Why did I feel the same way after I had that dream in second grade? But this was a female not a male. And who was talking to me telling me what to do? The voice was much clearer. It sounded like *Fantasy*, I thought. I felt powerful and in control and I was good at something? I'm all twisted inside now. I can't tell anyone.

Being brought up in church I knew how they felt and I dared not seek someone to help me with my questions. If I did they would have put me on the altar and had me tarrying until Jesus' return.

I couldn't tell anyone this incident so I held it in and pushed it down until it eventually, I thought, would go away. I had been told so many times that no man would ever want to marry a fat girl that it was embedded in the lining of my very soul. Maybe I was being shown a different way to live. But now was not the time to make sense of what I'd just done. I was too busy trying not to be noticed, fight my way through school, deal with peers at church as well as the adults and maintain my sanity. With this added to the mix was a bit much. I had to push it down into a neat box somewhere inside of me. Just like everything else in my life I was trying to hold down, but it eventually was going to come up but when and where was the question.

When and where was the question.

MASK/Behaviors: Pseudo-Power, People Pleasing, Afraid of Femininity, Questioning Gender Role

UNMASK: Opportunities will present themselves to children who have been traumatized and extremely rejected by those closest to them. These will not be the opportunities you want for them, but a child just wants someone to show them they're worthy of love, to give love, and be loved. It matters not after a while where it comes from. They just want to know what love is. Enough of these opportunities presented to them you will find their attention diverting from what once should have been a safe environment to the "other" who will give them what they want. But again, it may not be what you wanted for your child.

Sex is a powerful tool. It can be used to make one feel in charge, affirming the wounded, and making worthy the unloved. This moment in my life did define a time that was forthcoming. I shoved this memory way down in a place where I did not know the name. But just like anything that goes down eventually will wait and bide its time to come up when you're not looking and it did.

Pay attention to who your child is around. Enough said.

Your Memories of
Pictures, Snapshots, or
Fragments
(Write, Draw, Doodle,
Color, Scribble)

26

Signed, Sealed & Delivered

Finally, the last day of school couldn't come quick enough. We all anxiously waited to see if we passed to the next grade. She called us one by one to her desk to read it in her grade book. I passed, thank God!!! Then she passed out certificates for attendance, academic achievements, creative and artistic contributions to the class. I just knew I would get one for art, but it was between me and a Hispanic girl. Mrs. Cameron made the class choose which one would receive the certificate. She campaigned for the other girl like it was a presidential election. She walked around the classroom showing off her artwork and telling the class all what she had done for various events. I had nothing against my classmate. She was actually very nice, but I wanted a certificate. I coerced my classmates into voting for me because I clearly saw in their eyes, they were siding with Mrs. Cameron. I did the doe eyes with some classmates and with others I balled my fist. It was a sad win. When school was over I tore the certificate up before I got home. It was not given out of appreciation, but fear and pity. I just wanted to get home and far away from Charles R. Drew School. But what I really wanted was to be far away from Mrs. Cameron, she hated me as I her, twice as much.

I realized that year I knew many people, but I had one friend. I knew I wasn't nor would I ever be a part of any group in school or have long lasting friendships. I wore the

185

label "not good enough" and I was judged. I bore the mark of Cain. I was *Rejection's* baby.

🦗 *MASK/Behaviors: I didn't just have the behaviors grounded in me, I was becoming the embodiment of* **REJECTION, SHAME, FEAR, BULLY, PERFECT, ANGER, RAGE, ENVY, COMPARISON, COMPETITION, JEALOUSY, EMBARRASSMENT, SELF-PITY, VICTIM, PASSIVE/AGGRESSIVE, HURT, PAIN, DECEIVER, SCHIZOPHRENIA, PEOPLE PLEASER, DRAMA QUEEN, ATTENTION GETTER, SELF-HATRED, SELF-REJECTION, ABANDON, SEXUAL CONFUSION, NEEDY, MURDERER, OFFENSE, KILLER OF DREAMS, RELIGIOUS HYPOCRITE, PARTY BUZZ KILLER, JUDGMENT, CRITICAL, MANIPULATOR, CONTROL, INSENSITIVE, REBELLION AND UNCOMPASSIONATE,** *and all the others you have read. Each behavior, and each mask my soul was almost covered with them, and my authentic self to tired, was nearly convinced to accept its fate.*

UNMASK: This is not to say that all those in authority will have ill-will against children. But please discern wisely when your child is consistently making statements about an authority figure. Take an active part in your child's life, whether it be in academia, religious affiliation, recreational, social, etc. No one should have more of an influence in your child's life than you and make sure you are not agreeing with the authority figure because of your own unresolved issues or limiting belief system. Check your past to see if these areas are dead or alive. Pray for a more balanced, wise outlook in all areas of your life. Remember, you are responsible for your child's physical and emotional being. Their mindset is greatly molded by those who they spend the most time with. Make sure it is one who wants the child to be all they can be and to live out their purpose in a healthy and balanced mindset. But first make sure you are emotionally healthy or at least aware of your own belief system. If you recognize it needs some readjusting then by all means work on it. It is imperative that you are pursuing a healthy and balanced mindset so your child can have a positive example that no other negative force can penetrate.

Your Memories of
Pictures, Snapshots, or
Fragments
(Write, Draw, Doodle,
Color, Scribble)

27

Pokey Arm

June is promotion month to the next level of Sunday school classes and it's another 3:30 p.m. service called Children's Day. The teachers decided who was to be promoted to the next level. I was being promoted to the Junior class from the Primary class. There were two sisters that taught each level. The Primary class teacher, I really liked her because during this particular time in my life she was nice to me. In my teen years was a different story. I was going to her sister's class right along with the girl who flipped me the bird during the Christmas program. She was only a year older than me, but still was not old enough to be promoted to the next class. Her birthday fell after the cut-off date. I was disappointed, but what could I do?

Every Sunday there was an order in how the class was conducted. The teacher would read the introduction of the Sunday school lesson and then she would ask for volunteers to read each paragraph depending on how many were in class that day. I liked to read. I really did. But what I didn't like was being used as an example. Let me explain. All the other girls in the class were small framed. I was the only chubby girl. For some reason the teacher would take my arm, hold it, and around my wrist area or on my lower arm beneath the elbow, she would take her steel ballpoint pen and poke it in different places. Honestly, I can't remember why and what she used me as an example for. I was afraid to tell my Mama, because I didn't want to get my teacher in trouble, but it was getting ridiculous and it hurt. After many Sunday's I decided my arms had taken enough abuse and I told my Mama.

The next Sunday my Mama approached her and told her not to take her pen and poke my arm anymore. After my Mama spoke with her, she came into her room, closed the door and glared at me with a pissed and a mocking look on her face. The look said *how you dare tell on me*. Normally she would have read the introduction, but she asked the bird finger girl to read. Everyone in the class knew something was wrong. The classroom was cold and distant. I felt a little bad, but really why did she feel that she had the right to touch me, poke me, whatever, without my consent. I didn't want to read. I didn't want to be in her class. I didn't want to be in Sunday school. I didn't want to be at church.

Church, God, family and the people who claimed to *Love* me all felt like *Pain*. *Pain* and *Love* were synonymous and it was confusing. They embarrassed me about my weight and used my Mama as leverage to make me do things in church that I really didn't want to do. That was not love. It was *Mean* and an abuse of authority.

My views on family, religion and education were based on the adage "do as I say and not as I do." Their show of love was based on *Shame* and *Pain*. At the end of Sunday school class that day she asked me why I didn't tell her it hurt when she poked my arm. I asked her why she didn't poke any of the other girls? To add insult to injury she stated she didn't use the other girl's arms because they didn't have meat on them like me. Then the coup de grâce

190

she said she didn't think it'd hurt me because I was fat. And her point was because I was chubby? I didn't hurt like everyone else, especially if you took a steel ballpoint pen and poked my arm? What kind of thinking was that? It was the behavior of an abuser who at one time was abused.

I attended church with a hatred that grew every time I entered the doors. But I kept shoving that hate and all my real feelings down inside of me because I knew God wouldn't like me being that way. Like He really didn't know what was going on inside of me? Yeah. Right. I sacrificed my authenticity so I could be left alone by God and man.

🌿 *MASK/Behaviors: Self-Hatred, Fear of people, Fear of those in authority, Hoarder of emotions, Hatred of church, Self-Loathing, Murderer, Anger, Shame, Self-Rejection, No-body, a No-thing*

UNMASK: My real self was nearly gone. I was closing the door on the real me and everyone else. I operated like a toy robot when turned on. I did open up to certain people, but not a lot. I couldn't tell them everything about me or how I really felt. I felt like a snake slithering up to people pretending to be a part of the clique when I knew deep down inside I was not a part of a clique or life for that matter. It just felt good to be around people. I felt like some-body. It was a moment that the no-body went somewhere else.

Hitting me, poking me, later became slapping me, punching me in my young adult years. I didn't even have the courage to fight back. Telling on my teacher was a rare moment. She was very close to my family. I was so afraid to tell my Mama but the pokes really hurt. But what I hated was I became more and more like the abuser as I grew up. There were other forms I took on that I used to hurt

191

people like Silence. I became Sullen and Withdrawn to draw people into making them see about my welfare. I didn't know it until I began to read books on Anger, Rejection, Low Self-esteem, etc. Each book I read seemed as if the author watched me grow up. Each scenario guided me, informed me into what I'd become and it explained the type of people I drew to me and the devastation of some close relationships. Mainly I saw my behavior in black and white. Yes, it hurt the Truth, but I was determined to heal, by any means necessary. I have been just as insensitive to myself, and others, as to those who hit me. I became the "monster." It's like becoming a vampire. Some may not want to bite you and others like the feeling of power they get when they bite an innocent person. It only takes one bite and I was bit by generations of rejected people and I in turn bit other people through my dysfunctional behavior. I didn't want to bite but I was operating off of someone else's bite and those before them and so on...

If you are hearing me, stop, and really examine your relationships, your life. It will tell you things you may have overlooked, shoved into a place inside that you forgot where, or put aside thinking it was not worth remembering. But the Truth of the matter is the smallest thing could be the one thing that turns the light on and shows you the way out of your emotionally locked room. Remember who poked you, even the most intimate, gory, horrifying details so you and generations after, you won't remain in the same locked room.

Your Memories of
Pictures, Snapshots, or
Fragments
(Write, Draw, Doodle,
Color, Scribble)

28

Church Camp Hell

Normally I liked church camp. I'd go just to get away from home. I participated in some of the activities, but mostly I stayed to myself. I watched everyone else have their kind of fun and I had mine such as it was.

In the summer before I became a sixth grader in the fall I had the privilege to go to camp twice. The first time I went I met some really nice girls from Kokomo, Indiana that befriended me and we had fun. Well, they were coming back for the youth conference in three weeks and I was too.

The pre-teens and teenagers from my church rode down in the director's car but she was not staying. My relative, the leader of the teenagers, would chaperon the entire group. The girl who shot the bird at the 3:30 p.m. Christmas program was going with us too. The ride down I kept my eyes open because I didn't trust any of the girls I was with. We finally made it after getting lost a couple of times. I couldn't wait to see my friends I met earlier at camp.

We checked in and went to find vacant beds. It was late and I knew I wasn't going to find my friends that evening. I purposely wanted a bed at the end of a row, so I wouldn't be near any of the girls I came with. I found one, put my bags on the bed and went to the bathroom. When I came back my bags had been moved to another bed that was surrounded by their beds. Talk about the spider(s) and the fly, I barely slept that night. I was too damn scared. Not all of them were mean and vindictive, but the birdfinger girl swayed the others. She was excellent in manipulating situations that blamed me. She enjoyed getting me in trouble with my relative to hear her loudly berate me in public. I was their entertainment. I went to sleep after they did and I woke up early the next morning to find my real friends and get away from the people I came with.

In the bathroom, I saw my girlfriends. I was so happy to see them. We decided to eat breakfast together after we dressed and cleaned our area. It was mandatory that we cleaned our area where we slept and made our beds. I showered, dressed really quickly, made my bed, swept my area and flew downstairs to wait for my friends. This dormitory was huge it held two hundred plus women with cots as far as the eye could see. I checked again in my mind to make sure everything was done. Dirty clothes in their bag, bed made, and the floor swept. Yes! Everything was all done.

About thirty minutes later Ms. Birdfinger came downstairs to tell me my relative wanted to see me. I quickly went over the list in my head of the chores I completed before going downstairs. What did I forget? I heard a vicious snicker from Ms. Birdfinger and underneath her breath, she said, "You are in trouble." *In trouble?! About what?* I thought. I did my mental checklist again. Everything was covered. I made sure of that – everything.

The closer I got to my cot I saw the coven surrounding it. My relative was in the midst glaring at me. I looked underneath my bed and I saw all this dirt, dust, and debris. My eyes opened in shock because I knew I swept that morning and made my bed. The accusations flew out of my relative's mouth. I told her no, I emphatically told her no. I swept and made up my bed before I left. She bellowed out the names *Lazy* and *Trifling* like they were God-given. I told her again that I got up early and cleaned. That is why I was downstairs. And again, she screamed even louder which attracted a larger audience. I looked at the coven of people in the circle surrounding me, taunting me with their eyes. Her words became more vicious as spittle flew out of her mouth with each word. Everything began to move in slow motion as my heart beat in my ears. My mouth closed. I knew it was useless to defend myself. I had been down this road before with her from a little girl and she was always determined to get the last word in no matter what.

My head turned toward the back of the building. I saw a lady sitting there watching the whole situation. She appeared to have tears in her eyes coupled with a look of pity. For that moment in time at the stake burning I was comforted by her presence. Amongst the words, the hurtful words I bowed and picked up my bedclothes and began to make up the bed once more. Afterwards, I picked up the broom and swept until the debris was once again in the receptacle. Ms. Birdfinger hissed and told me I missed some dirt. I picked it up as well.

My relative wouldn't even listen to my side of the story. Stupid me. Why should I have thought differently? She never did. She always sided with those who were against me. When she would hurt me at home, I went underneath the stairwell and killed her in so many ways. That was the

196

only place I had the courage to meet her in combat and I always won.

That morning in front of two hundred plus females she shot names at me to embarrass me and make herself feel powerful. But when she did that, I saw one face in the crowd, a lady, who seemed purposely planted by God to tell me that it was Him. He knew the truth and saw the situation. While writing this story I saw the face of that woman in my mind's eye. He let me know He was there. And all these years I thought He could have cared less. I still wished someone would have stood up for me because standing up for me was futile. I stopped trying to defend myself. I stopped talking. My voice was only audible in my head where no one could hear me. I was afraid of everyone and everything. I couldn't tell the difference between friend and enemy. But this moment I can let the hatred and bitterness toward God and the relative go. He was there and my relative, I'd learned later, was trapped in her own emotional prison of *Rejection*.

🦋 *MASK/Behaviors: Shame, Desperate for friendships, Hatred of females, Embarrassment, Avoid conflict, Hatred of family, Murderer, Confusion*

UNMASK: If you are a parent or guardian and still haunted by Ridicule, Embarrassment, or Shame as a child, then more than likely you will do the same to your child as was done to you. In fact, it is safe to say that if you Embarrass or Shame your child, you are not seeing them in the present. You think you are getting revenge on the person who shamed you in your past. Your child is paying for your emotional wounds and that is more confusing to the child as to why they are being abused. If you Hate yourself, then you can't love your child. There will be a wound from the past that will rear its head telling you it's not gone. This must be dealt with. No matter how you may suppress your past hurts, they will lay dormant until the opportune time. And when they come forth, usually it is in the presence of innocent ones who remind you of the person(s) who hurt you or of yourself being abused. "Physician, heal thyself." Root issues must be acknowledged to self- first. That is half the battle. Your child does not deserve to be the punching bag of your past wounds.

Your Memories of
Pictures, Snapshots, or
Fragments
(Write, Draw, Doodle,
Color, Scribble)

29

The Last Straw

The last straw came when I was walking back from piano lessons. I got home and my mother was there alone. I noticed her mellow demeanor. She had been drinking. The relative who came to live with us had gone downtown to the annual sidewalk sale. It was extremely hot outside and I was really tired. The back of my legs was hurting as always and I just wanted to rest. Shortly thereafter the relative came back with her bag of goodies. After showing us what she bought she asked my mother could I go back with her. *I* didn't ask to go back with her. And what made her think I wanted to go downtown? My mother turned to me and asked did I want to go. I liked what she bought for herself, but I wasn't interested in going back with her. I told her no. That is when the names started again. *Fat, lazy, trifling* came out of my relative's mouth and sadly my mother agreed with her. I went to the bathroom and cut on the water, bowed my head and let the tears flow. I heard my relative leave and my mother came to the bathroom and told me to unlock the door. She started taunting me and teasing me about what I was missing by not going downtown. But the truth of the matter was I didn't care. I was tired of people assuming for me that they knew how I felt or thought as if what I felt and thought wasn't valid.

All I wanted was to go into my bedroom and lay down, but she blocked my way. I slid along the wall to the floor and pretended I didn't hear what she was saying to me. She took her foot and slightly kicked me. That is when I went off and screamed "Hell, why don't you ask her to be your daughter?" She mockingly laughed at me and asked, "Are you jealous?" Her touch made my skin crawl and that feeling continued until the day she died. In fact, it was not until recently that I don't cringe as much when people in general touch me. I had to learn to listen to my Spirit tell me when people are playing with me or wanting to hurt me when they touch me. But I admit I still don't like it when people like to hit when they are talking to me. If you gently touch me, I'm okay with that.

My mother had a chance that day to redeem herself from all her silent moments when she allowed *Rage* from another close relative to bellow at me. But she acquiesced and came into agreement with the other shameful voices. No one else was there to interfere, interrupt, co-sign or thrash me with their pain. She could freely, openly, without *Fear* defend me, protect me, shelter me with her vast vocabulary but she didn't. Her mocking words, tone and laughter joined by the invisible chorus of verbal lynches extended the killing blow to that last bit of *Hope* I held on to for dear life. I knew then beyond a shadow of a doubt I was on my own. Family, my family was never going to protect me. Berating me and having an audience satisfied something deep inside of them. And my mother sealed that knowledge with a slight kick to my leg like you would do to a dog.

MASK/Behaviors: Invisible, Self-Rejection, Anger, Self-Hatred, Rage, Schizophrenia, Loner, Low Self-Esteem, Abuser/Abused, Emotional Dishonesty, Hatred of family, Church and God, Authentic self is dead

(Rejection and its family members all grounded and sealed in my wounded soul.)

UNMASK: How can a parent compare their child to another? I couldn't understand what was wrong with me. Why was I never good enough to be me, whoever that was? I didn't know me anymore. Did I ever? Calling a child out of their name, comparing your child to another will certainly bring forth a mild case or full blown schizophrenia. When a child is daydreaming all the time or not doing well in school, attention deficit, rebellion, extremely shy, talk to themselves more than other people, pay close attention to how you've treated them.

I knew a woman that when she whipped her child she never used her hands. She used wooden cooking spoons to hit her on her thighs and legs. She never hit above that area. I asked her why. She told me, "that hands are used for holding and hugging to show your love. If I hit her with them and then try to embrace her later she will back away from me because she won't know if I'm going to hit her or hug her. It is confusing for the child and also leads to abuse because she will think if a man hits her that is love." From that point on I understood clearly why I hated being touched. I back up from people a little when they come close to me or they playfully hit me even if I knew them. Now I can approach to hug other people because I'm in control and I'm not going to harm them.

Pay even closer attention to how you were treated in your early years. The apple doesn't fall too far from the tree. What wounds you deny your child will internalize. It comes to a point

202

where your child won't remember who they are and will emotionally clock out and all is left is a shell. Columbine and other unreported and reported situations that happen daily are nothing more than an esteem that has been damaged or destroyed to the point the child feels that no one cares and is invisible to the world as the world is invisible to them. If a child grows to adulthood without consistent healthy encouragement or affirming words to strengthen their esteem, and without divine intervention, the same mindset remains –uncaring and invisible to self and others. The manifestations, then become alcoholism, mind altering drugs, over the counter drugs, physical abuse, a cutter (cut your own skin to release pain), OCD, bi-polar, obesity, bulimia, anorexia, aggressive interest in pornography, constantly working, extremely independent spirit, so many ways. And some people you can look at them and see their pain. It's not always the homeless person on the street, some live in houses, but their house is not a home. Please don't compare your child. Remember, they are a little image of you, and there lies the problem. Selah (PAUSE and calmly think of that)

Obituary

Lana M. Hooks
May 18, 1962-July? 1973

Lana Marie Hooks was born May 18, 1962, in Gary, Indiana, at Mercy Hospital at 12:53 a.m., to Annie K. Boyde and Larnell Hooks Sr. She weighed 5 lbs. and some odd ounces, which is small for a baby, but alas, that would be the last time the word "small" would pertain to her body.

Her mother wanted to name her Morgan but there was a beautiful young lady she and Mama knew named Lana Marie. She was beautiful inside and out and Lana's Mama thought that name would be better suited for her granddaughter.

It's funny how a meaning of a name can define the character and personality of a person unless a person's esteem has been crushed and replaced to believe someone else's reality.

Lana is a derivative of *Alana* (English) which means "precious." In Russian another derivative is Svetlana "light" and in Hawaiian it is "afloat" or "calm as still water." Lana in Latin means "wool," Gaelic it is "rock," German it is "beautiful and fair," Greek it is "shining light," and in Irish "child, attractive and peaceful." Hooks her surname meant, "Dweller on a bend of a river, road or ridge." The meanings of her name implied a beautiful, peaceful and calm person, one who was strong but she was treated and acted the exact opposite.

As a baby Lana was loved, but after the age of three her family's love was shown in hurtful words and sometimes physical abuse. Growing up left her without love, self-esteem and emotionally severed family ties. All she ever wanted was for them to love and accept her as she was chubby, fat, short, fair skin, intelligent in her own way and creative. But most of all she wanted them to protect her.

Instead, inflicted by their own shame they used their acidic words to make her feel ashamed of herself physically and mentally. They called her fat, so many times until she developed a Body Image Disorder. The hatred towards her body and jealous of thin girls grew to insurmountable covetousness until she didn't see her "fearfully and wonderfully made" body anymore.

In fact, in her mind, she was invisible and also to the world. She walked among the living as a zombie who obeyed to a fault those who verbally punched and on occasion physically did the same. Her authentic thoughts, feelings, ideas, creativity, emotions died along with her voice. The way she walked, talked and even wrote was copied from peers her family showed fondness towards. Her desires became whoever was around her to avoid conflict and disagreement.

Her mind, even if she tried to be herself, could only agree with whoever had the most power and clout. Being a hypocrite, coward, joker and the victim were a way of life for her to cope without being seen and or noticed. It was quiet in her fantasy world, everyone got along, no fussing, fighting and anger was definitely not allowed. In reality she didn't even allow herself to be angry. If she became angry she found a way to justify the abuser's treatment towards her and blamed herself. Just to keep the peace (as her insides churned in private and at boiling level) she shoved those feelings deep down inside while cataloguing every crime scene and persons involved. Her stomach swelled because it couldn't contain the growing files of crimes committed not just by others, but unbeknownst to her by her as well. Peace had to be maintained at all cost even if it meant she lied, manipulated, deceived and gave up her authentic self for the sake of not hearing another person call her fat, lazy and trifling. She died the day her mother had a chance to defend her, protect her, and accept her, but chose not to. She had just turned eleven.

Ashes to ashes and dust to dust her emotional and behavioral authentic self we commit to a place only God knows where it's at.

Your Memories of
Pictures, Snapshots, or
Fragments
(Write, Draw, Doodle,
Color, Scribble)

Concludes with a Few Additions

From the womb until fifth grade I fought as much as I could, but that moment with my mother I literally gave up the ghost. The memory of her foot touching my skin produced such a disdain in me that I cringe when people touch me whether it is pleasant or harmful.

I regret that I never accepted my mother's touch. I tried to feel comfortable when she did touch me, but I recoiled every time. Other relatives that had emotionally scarred me died with the death of my childhood years as well. My Mama and my siblings were the only ones that I had an emotional attachment to.

My Mama was not an overly affectionate person, but she did listen to me and talked to me. She was the one I confided in and cried to while she tried to convince me by God's word to not hate my mother. But little did she know, or, maybe she did, I was beyond hatred. I was indifferent. I felt not one way or the other. My emotional investment was in my Mama and when her health was failing I created a world where I wanted to nurse her back to health. But sad to say that didn't happen. One of our last conversations was her telling me every last detail of what was going to physically happen to my mother and my role I was to play in the hellish nightmare that was to come. She prophetically spoke to me, but at that time I wasn't aware of things like that. And yes, everything happened as she stated it to me that day sitting in her infamous rocking chair and her lying on the bed.

This is not the relationship I desired with my family. I wanted us to be a close, loving, supportive family. I never could understand why we fought, yelled, raped our esteem with vicious words, and seldom listened to each other. I intensely envied families that showered their children with affection, paid attention to their unique voices, listened to them, supported their endeavors and just plain old loved them. I often wondered what was wrong with my family. Why we couldn't exhibit those traits to each other or even acknowledge them?

Stages of a Child

As an adult in counseling I became interested in family dynamics and dysfunctions. I read everything but what caught my eye were sibling placement and the process of the formative years of children by Erik Erikson, a psychiatrist, at the Child Development Institute, in 1956.

The formative years of a child, is where hope, will, purpose, and competence from infancy through junior high school are developed. My years according to this model were the complete opposite.

He states there are eight stages or eight phases of man. For the purpose of my memoir I've expressed four of them that describe and defend why it is extremely imperative to leave a legacy to our children of a healthy emotional mindset.

Each stage is regarded by Erikson as a "psychosocial crisis," which arises and demands resolution before the next stage can be satisfactorily negotiated. These stages are conceived in an almost architectural sense: satisfactory learning and resolution of each crisis is necessary if the child is to manage the next and subsequent ones satisfactorily, just as the foundation of a house is essential to the first floor, which in turn must be structurally sound to support and the second story, and so on.

1. Learning Basic Trust versus Basic Mistrust (Hope)
Chronologically, this is the period of infancy through the first one or two years of life. The child, well - handled, nurtured, and

loved, develops trust and security and a basic optimism. Badly handled, he becomes insecure and mistrustful.

2. Learning Autonomy versus Shame (Will)

The second psychosocial crisis, Erikson believes, occurs during early childhood, probably between about 18 months or 2 years and 3½ to 4 years of age. The "well - parented" child emerges from this stage sure of himself, elated with his new found control, and proud rather than ashamed. Autonomy is not, however, entirely synonymous with assured self - possession, initiative, and independence but, at least for children in the early part of this psychosocial crisis, includes stormy self - will, tantrums, stubbornness, and negativism. For example, one sees may 2 year olds resolutely folding their arms to prevent their mothers from holding their hands as they cross the street. Also, the sound of "NO" rings through the house or the grocery store.

3. Learning Initiative versus Guilt (Purpose)

Erikson believes that this third psychosocial crisis occurs during what he calls the "play age," or the later preschool years (from about 3½ to, in the United States culture, entry into formal school). During it, the healthily developing child learns: (1) to imagine, to broaden his skills through active play of all sorts, including fantasy (2) to cooperate with others (3) to lead as well as to follow. Immobilized by guilt, he is: (1) fearful (2) hangs on the fringes of groups (3) continues to depend unduly on adults and (4) is restricted both in the development of play skills and in imagination.

4. Industry versus Inferiority (Competence)

Erikson believes that the fourth psychosocial crisis is handled, for better or worse, during what he calls the "school age," presumably up to and possibly including some of junior high school. Here the child learns to master the more formal skills of life: (1) relating with peers according to rules (2) progressing from free play to play that may be elaborately structured by rules and may demand formal teamwork, such as baseball and (3) mastering social studies, reading, arithmetic. Homework is a necessity, and the need for self-discipline increases yearly. The child who, because of his successive and successful resolutions of earlier psychosocial crisis, is trusting, autonomous, and full of initiative will learn easily enough to be industrious. However, the mistrusting child will doubt the future. The shame - and guilt-filled child will experience defeat and inferiority (http://www. childdevelopmentinfo.com/development/erickson.shtml).

The only other vital key in my opinion that was missing from this formula was the spiritual aspect. As I stated in the beginning words carry an energy of life or death. It transmits from the giver to the receiver the intent or motive of the heart. If the words are meant to hurt, they will do so as well as the opposite. And those words spoken to my mother penetrated my body (fetus) and brought with it their negative motive. Professor Erikson's first phase is to learn trust or mistrust **after** the child is born. But I learned mistrust **in** the womb and different entities, i.e., *Rejection*, etc., grew as I did with each scenario of my development.

Your Memories of
Pictures, Snapshots, or
Fragments
(Write, Draw, Doodle,
Color, Scribble)

Shake That Tree

It is so important to understand your family tree. My sister has a saying that I laugh at but it is so true. She tells anyone who is thinking about taking their relationship to marriage status to, "Shake that tree, and shake it hard." Her movements are comical when she says it but I hear the seriousness of the tone in her voice. You must know your lineage emotionally, physically, relationally, socially, mentally, spiritually, and their sexuality. Why? Because unresolved issues of previous generations coupled with yours will be transmitted to your womb if you decide to have or already have children. Children will have enough to contend with in their lifetime. To bear the task of burdens before them on top of what they will experience is too much and NOT FAIR!

Not every issue will be conquered and won overnight, but at least you can begin to assemble your arsenal of weapons, i.e., counseling, prayer, reading self-help books, meditation, etc., to combat those negative belief systems and thought patterns that you know for sure you don't want passed to your child. And for those who have children it is not too late to change your way of rearing and transform your mind to execute new thought patterns to form new belief systems which will manifest into a healthy behavior.

For those who may not want children do not feel ashamed of your decision. I didn't want to have children either until I began to get honest with myself. From a young girl sitting under that stairwell, I told God or whoever was listening in the cosmos that I was never going to get married or have children. I knew I would be an abusive mother and a horrible spouse to living beings that didn't deserve my unhealthy emotional behavior. I remember thinking with such determination NEVER will I hurt a child, my child, because they didn't ask to be born (learned later we all ask to be born - another book). And to be with a man that I knew I would nag, or, talk to like he was a child, and possibly physically abuse (some women in my family have done it). I resounded loudly within my mind. NO!

My biological clock was a time bomb in my thirties, but I refused to give in to it. I had to honestly question if my reason and belief were authentic as to why I didn't want to have children or get married. No! It was all because of what I'd experienced from the womb until I was ten years old and was told that no man would marry me because I was fat. But the reality still stood if I had children at an early age I know I would have abused them. I knew me; I knew the cloth I was stitched into. But if you know for certain that children are not a part of your journey because you know who you are now or will be, or, if there is a fear of someone else's reality intruding on your conscience decision then stand by your word. Like in the movie "Poltergeist" when the little lady said assuredly, "This house is clean." Make sure your emotions, thought patterns and belief systems are in alignment to take care of you first then you will know when it is emotionally healthy and safe to desire children.

Despicable Me

From the womb until ten years of age as my emotions, behavior and authentic self were crushed by abusive words a new mask took its place until I couldn't recognize myself in body, mind and soul. As a result, I stopped looking in the mirror at the age of ten. And when I did the only features I saw were my face, hair, hands and feet. That's all I needed to see. I knew I was fat and I didn't need to look at the middle part of me. I had been told enough times about my condition, like I was a leper, and it wasn't worth viewing. My body is disproportionate. In my eyes, I looked freakish (a word God does not like for me to use). I noticed the older I was becoming my feet and hands remained at the age of ten or, how my arms and legs start out small boned but the further you move up any of my limbs the weight is too heavy for my small frame. I learned later in life that if a person has been severely emotionally, physically and verbally traumatized as a child their bodies will manifest a disfigurement in several ways. I remained the height I was in fifth grade or ten years of age. I never grew any taller than that. If you look at my picture posted in the middle of this book you will see that my legs were long in comparison to my torso. I was supposed to have been at least five feet, five inches tall (5'5"). I expanded outward not upward.

My skin has hair in places that shouldn't be for a woman. Besides the keloid on my ear, they surfaced on other parts of my body as well. And the sad part is I don't remember when they appeared. I literally stopped looking at my body. I hated to see that it didn't look like other girls my age.

Being told more than enough times from those with dirty breaths that a man would not want or marry me were constant reminders that led me to be socially immature, Body Image Disorder, and confusion about my sexuality.

I didn't have the normal teenage lifestyle of dating, going to dances, sports events, talent shows or class functions. At home I played an adult's role. I was trying to survive an emotionally dysfunctional haunted house. I was scared for my siblings and me. My baby brother, who is now deceased, called me mama for a while. I was no longer Lana the sister. I was mother to all of us, including my mother. There were days when I didn't know if we were going to eat, the utilities were off most of the time, and I could intuitively detect when they were. Most of all I wondered when my mother went out with her oldest brother when she'd come home. I lived in constant upheaval and fear of the unknown. Fantasy constantly fed me her stories as I pretended to be someone else in my painful world. Physically, I was gaining more weight. I lied to my family and other people consistently to make them think I had many friends in school. But truthfully, I was alone most of the time or with a female at school that I allowed to emotionally abuse me as well.

Body Image Disorder in a nutshell, is a disease of the mind. It is not only how and what you think of your body, but your identity is wrapped up in the way your body looks. As you have read I learned to hate my body. We **must** realize whether large or small we are uniquely designed. We are a blueprint that only the Creator can reveal to the creation the how, the why, and what is good for us socially, spiritually, and so much more. In addition He can reveal to us the exercises and food to keep us healthy and what fits our body frame to make our bodies breathe. But most of all what thoughts are beneficial to maintain emotional and mental healthiness.

Your Memories of
Pictures, Snapshots, or
Fragments
(Write, Draw, Doodle,
Color, Scribble)

No Regrets

My confusion about my sexuality was not addressed again until my thirties. I was with a guy who had been incarcerated, but he was working at a reputable establishment. One night and for no apparent reason he beat me like a child. He beat me after we just had sex. He also laughed at my body after and sometimes during sex. After that horrible turn of event, I chose to be in a relationship with a female. I don't regret it. Remember what happened when I was ten well it came back twenty years later and this time I willingly walked into it. Why? It was my belief system in motion in being told no man would ever want to be with a fat girl like me. It was a self-fulfilling prophecy. And after being hit by this man (and another in college) and not ever having a healthy relationship with a man, I said why not? Let's try this and see where it goes. But I learned, and this is my lesson and journey, that a relationship, whether same sex or heterosexual if you go into without authentically knowing who you are emotionally then the relationship is built upon emotional dishonesty. I **made** myself like being with a female. And again, I don't regret it, but I knew it wasn't for me. I was operating out of a wounded soul and it was not fair to the person I was with or me.

Your Memories of
Pictures, Snapshots, or
Fragments
(Write, Draw, Doodle,
Color, Scribble)

Hope

Conquering the negative, dysfunctional belief system in these area's takes time, prayer and trust in my Creator. And even believing that my Creator was on my side was a whole other battle I gradually conquered which was not easy. Even when I didn't necessarily believe that the Creator would help me, I hoped He would. Hope was all I had. I read about others who lived through their nightmares and came out a brand new person and I rigorously prayed that the Creator would do the same for me. That's all I had was hope, and that is what kept me from committing suicide on several occasions.

A tiered generational belief system of low self-worth in my family, men and women; coupled with the hurt from their own childhood; add another layer of derogatory words on one's physical image (females); false perfection ideals; pressure to belong; pressure to live up to society's image; desiring to feel like one of the girls; and strongly wanting a handsome boy/man to be with; wanting me and not be ashamed of me; poverty mindset; feeling powerless and weak as a female, I was in one word – tired.

Was this how I wanted my life to be? Did I want to hate my body? Did I want to be confused about my sexuality? No! My low self-esteem forbade me to think that a nice, handsome man my age would want someone like me. At one point I actually was going to resign myself to be with just married men, but like I said Divine Intervention shut that door. This is what I want.

I want a man to really like me. I want to be married. I want the healthy longevity of couples, like Ossie Davis and Ruby Dee, who made a conscious decision to make their relationship work. I want my spouse to be an educated thug. That is a man who is academic smart and knows how to speak and behave from the boardroom to the streets. I want us to travel, work in our community, and be a part of a greater plan to make a change. If it is not in the cards for me to have children, then I want to work with children and offer them a safe place to just be. This is how I want my life to be and now I know I can still have that life. It may be modified, but I can still have it now that my emotional and behavioral authenticity is being unearthed in me from a place truly in my Creator's vision and thoughts of me. I am learning on a daily basis to love me, all of me, the good, bad, ugly and indifferent. I now know I have options and I can change or transform my belief system at any time. It's up to me. There are many routes one can take in life to live, and live emotionally and behaviorally healthy.

Love Never Fails

I implore you to once again love your child the way the *Creator* made them. Children just want to be accepted, protected, and loved for who they are and not molded into mini'-me's of their parents or guardians. Growing up in confusion, with suicidal tendencies, self-hatred and other murderous thoughts, and after all is said and done settling for whatever life brings is not living. This is death! Change your thoughts you can change your life. Do that for you and your child/children.

Your Memories of
Pictures, Snapshots, or
Fragments
(Write, Draw, Doodle,
Color, Scribble)

Church, God and Me: A Sad U Cee

Religion was my scapegoat. I hid behind religion. I was a Sadducee and Pharisee, haughty and self-righteous to the core, but I was on the down low, the worst kind. I tried to be the opposite of my mother. I wanted to be the good child, the perfect child, but in reality, I behaved as she did only without the excessive drinking. My drug of choice was smoking.

I **was** like those people in church that judged my mother and called her a whore for being pregnant out of wedlock, but I later found out they secretly had underground abortions. One of the first Black nurses in Gary told my mother this information to encourage her and also to let her know about the hypocrisy in the church. I understood why she shied away from church and drank to try and forget the words and treatment of those closest to her. There is nothing like a church hurt. It's just like family when you get hurt the cut is deep and not so easily forgiven.

I knew the "religious" language to a tee. I appeared to be perfect, but as you've read I was a hot mess and going to church out of habit. Like I said there I was sitting in church hating God, myself, my family and anyone who harmed me. I thought I was really hiding this from God. I still laugh at that. But years later, sitting in a church I belonged to at that time in Atlanta I sincerely asked God who I really was and to change me from this schizoid person I'd become. I also asked Him to refine my character and to make me a person of integrity.

226

Your Memories of
Pictures, Snapshots, or
Fragments
(Write, Draw, Doodle,
Color, Scribble)

You Do Get What You Ask For but You Don't Know How It Will Come

When you seek Truth, God, Consciousness, will show up in full form. OMG! This process has taught me how much I didn't know the Truth and how Truth works... LOL! I really thought I wasn't *that* dysfunctional. Right! I just thought it was a simple request for God to make me a person of integrity. I didn't realize until challenge after challenge, after a struggle, after a struggle that Truth goes all the way back to the origin of that belief system in the bloodline and unravels the damage it has done in all parts of the soul (mind, body, emotions). Some issues may take longer than others to be fully healed, but the beauty of liberation is you begin to wake up to be introduced to the real you, the authentic you. *Self-Acceptance, Honesty,* and *Transparency* become your best friends in *Self-Realization.* And it is an enlivening feeling, in fact, it is priceless. What you thought to fit in, be a part of, act like, look like, really doesn't matter. All that matters is you seeing yourself for the very first time. It really is like falling in love with someone who loves you for you, only it is yourself. Your authentic identity greets you and this time it stays. That is the greatest feeling in the world. If my story can veer you from taking the long route please do so. But as I stated before, I do realize for some people the long route will be your plight, just please minimize the time you will have to learn your lessons by being obedient to the process.

Your Memories of
Pictures, Snapshots, or
Fragments
(Write, Draw, Doodle,
Color, Scribble)

Soul Wounds

I've mentioned the soul, but not really explained the blows it takes and will live with until the body can't take it anymore. It will reveal the damage through sickness and dis-ease. The soul suffers the most devastation.

According to (http://dictionary.reference.com/browse/soul), the soul is *the principle of life, feeling, thought, and action in humans, regarded as a distinct entity separate from the body, and commonly held to be separable in existence from the body; the spiritual part of humans as distinct from the physical part.*

My soul (and body) are finally finding rest, peace and healing as I continue to walk out my life. The medical and spiritual community is flowing together to show a relationship of how toxic emotions as *Fear, Anxiety, and Stress* are the root cause of Hypertension, Diabetes and other autoimmune diseases. When the soul has been severely injured by traumatic events the nervous, musculoskeletal, circulatory, respiratory, gastrointestinal, integumentary, urinary, reproductive, and endocrine system have been crushed into like a head on truck collision. The body is extremely sensitive to stressful and traumatic situations. The women and men in my family know first-hand what toxic emotions can do to the body. The men in my family, including my father wrestled with Prostate Cancer twice and won. My oldest uncle had Dementia and my baby uncle had Lung Cancer both are deceased. The root causes I have read stem from *Self-Rejection, Self-Hatred and Guilt*. Other ailments in my family include Eczema, OCD, Obesity, Suicidal tendencies, Arthritis, Lower Back problems, Eating Disorders, Tuberculosis gene, and the Sickle Cell Gene. The younger generations of my family are prone to these diseases and it brings me to tears every time. To be emotionally, behaviorally and physically healthy is a birthright, a gift from the Creator. That is why I'm calling out the pink elephants in the room. There are too many and the weight of them crushes the very life out of families.

I believe to exist and not live authentically is the greatest crime to the soul. Counterfeit personalities, the mask I've revealed, and a belief system that is someone else's reality that has not been spoken aloud for fears of appearances and pride is a travesty.

My journey has not been easy and I can't believe I'm saying this, but it has been worth it. What keeps me going is always *Ms. Hope*. Hope that being open and transparent will destroy the words of yesteryear and birth in me words of how my Creator sees me no matter what frame of mind I am in. And my Creator never ceases to follow through in the darkest of moments to bring me those precious gifts to heal my esteem.

God's Breath: Mm… That Cool, Refreshing Drink

A new breath is blowing inside of me, a fresh, clean, pure and loving breath that is teaching me about forgiveness of self and others. Forgiveness shows me why people hurt people. I'm not going to say I forgave those who hurt me off the bat, but I didn't like *my* prison anymore. Unforgiveness kept me in an emotional prison that I couldn't take anymore. My soul cried for relief of its many wounds and it deserved to be set free. I begrudgingly at first forgave the other persons, but I didn't really mean it. But the more I said it, the more God revealed that person's soul wounds and my prayers became more genuine and sincere to me and the abuser.

What was revealed to me about the victimizer was the same toxic behavior I learned from them was in me too. I actually began to feel sorry for the other person and myself. Another challenging task was forgiving and loving myself. Even though the damage was done to me, I agreed with what they said, believed and sometimes refused to let go of the toxicity. For a moment I had to admit I was comfortable in my pain because it was familiar. Loving me was harder. I mean actually loving this body, this fat body that God loves unconditionally. Really looking at myself as how He sees me and not the words of hurt people. My eyesight, perception, and belief system needed to change, but I didn't know how. I've cried, screamed and hollered out to God to know how to love myself.

I want God to heal me of those imbedded false images and heal me but I was afraid. *Betrayal, mistrust,* and *hurt* were still between Him and me. I felt Him wrestling me and the urge to not speak to Him was losing. My soul opened my mouth and cried out in pain, a pain that I thought was gone. It wasn't. My soul cried out in anger and screamed my "ugly" thoughts, my raw thoughts of how I not only felt about me but Him as well. It's taken years for me to surrender. It has been a gradual surrender. Beginning with the surrendering to that second grade moment. I didn't think He wanted me to be my correct size. I thought He agreed with my family and those who talked about my weight. In fact, I thought He told them to say those mean words. I had to surrender to the Truth of how He sees me, how I see Him, my family's role, and my life.

I resolve daily to see myself as how God created me, to love my body in its present state. To love me the way I am, now, but to continue to walk my journey in learning to love the inner and outer weights off my body. No, I'm not all the way there, but I've made a decision to keep moving in that direction to fully, wholly love me.

I can't undo what has been done to me, but I can choose to let go of the pain and minute by minute do the work to maintain freedom in my soul. This is actually the most challenging part of letting go (yielding). It's like when you get a cut on your hand, it's quick and almost painless until you sit for a second then the pain comes. You wash it; pour peroxide which burns to cleanse the infection, put a band aid on it to not get it dirty, but underneath it, the cut burns, itches and new cells are growing while the skin is starting to mend itself. Healing hurts. It takes time for soul wounds to

233

be healed. But this is the gift you give to yourself to break free from the tentacles of your past and people. And it is a **must** to remember that this is a journey not a destination. If you do, you won't easily give up and settle when just another step will bring you closer to waking up and seeing another part of your emotional, behavioral authenticity. Each moment, not days, because all I can handle is the moment, are the steps I take to listen to the Truth, choose to wake up, choose to let go of the mask, breathe fresh air and learn how to really live authentically on all levels.

Your Memories of
Pictures, Snapshots, or
Fragments
(Write, Draw, Doodle,
Color, Scribble)

And Once Again...

   Parents pay strict attention to relatives, teachers, spiritual leaders, anyone in authority. Check them out thoroughly to see how your child responds in their presence. Small children are innocent and can show you better than tell you. Verbalizing their feelings come as they are growing up. Unless they have been denied or afraid to express their emotions honestly as author Steven Hein states, then they will let you know by actions.

   "Children start out emotionally honest. They express their true feelings freely and spontaneously. But the training to be emotionally dishonest begins at an early age. Parents and teachers frequently encourage or even demand that children speak or act in ways which are inconsistent with the child's true feelings. The child is told to smile when actually she is sad. She is told to apologize when she feels no regret. She is told to say "thank you," when she feels no appreciation. She is told to "stop complaining" when she feels mistreated. She may be told to kiss people good night when she would never do so voluntarily. She may be told it is "rude" and "selfish" to protest being forced to act in ways which go against her feelings... Also, children are told they can't use certain words to express themselves...In some cases the parent never allows the children to explain why they feel so strongly...As children become adolescents they begin to think more for themselves. They begin to speak out more, "talk back" more and challenge the adults around them. If these adults feel threatened, they are likely to defend themselves by invalidating the adolescent's feeling and perceptions...Through all of this the child and adolescent learns they can't be honest with their feelings. They

gradually stop being emotionally honest with their parents, their teachers, their friends and even themselves. They learn it just doesn't pay to express one's true feelings" (http://eqi. org/ehon.htm)

Please allow your child to be emotionally honest with words and actions. You can set the guidelines for them to show and tell it in a respectful manner. If you honor them, they will honor you. Unmet needs in you will be unmet needs of your child. You determine what kind of emotional legacy you pass to your child. Innocent lives depend on your choices.

I wrote my story for several reasons: one, if you are thinking about having children, or, if you do, think long and hard about what emotional legacy you want to pass to your child; two, if you have one or more than one child, remember they have their own personalities, seek Truth about each one and let Him explain to you how they are to be raised; three, with the information you gain about your child from Truth know that they can't be around everyone; fourth, to those in authoritative positions understand a child is a gift and you have the awesome responsibility to allow Truth to show you how to guide them. Lastly, I had to release these dirty breaths that I've held on to hide, justify, and blame, but I was really afraid and ashamed because I didn't know who I was and how to live - authentically.

I close in by saying some dirty breaths I haven't dispelled yet, but I **know** they are there and daily I seek my *Creator* who can remove those breaths. It does require work, patience, compassion, forgiveness for self and others and obedience. I may not like what Truth tells me to do some days, but in the end the *Emotional Freedom* my soul gains are priceless.

I suggest looking at the movie *It's a Wonderful Life* starring James Stewart. Your presence does influence not only your family, but your community, your town/city and events nationally and internationally. My eyes are being opened to see that if I had not been born so many lives would have been affected in ways that only Truth can reveal how precious our lives really are to Him.

I want children everywhere to know that families no matter what they are born into they are a treasure. And to the parents the *Creator* has given you a charge over His greatest creation – huemans – His children. Please, please understand, this is nothing to make light of. It's an honor and a privilege. Leave an emotional legacy that will build your child's esteem and not wound or bruise it. Don't let them have to start over. Give them a healthy emotional, behavioral running start in life.

Going forward, through all the moments of tears, pain, and confusion, I receive *Clarity* that opens my eyes and I breathe, my *Creator's* breath, a clean breath that tells me *I love you* and I answer back *I love me too.*

In Gratitude to my Creator,

Your Beautiful, Peaceful Daughter Lana

Your Memories of
Pictures, Snapshots, or
Fragments
(Write, Draw, Doodle,
Color, Scribble)

Endnotes

1. Academy of American Poets, "We Wear the Mask," http://www.poets.org/viewmedia. php/prmMID/15888.html. Accessed 2012.

Introduction

2. Wikipedia, s. v."Female genital mutilation," last modified February, 2010," http://en.wikipedia. org/wiki/Female_genital_cutting/.

3. Dream Moods A-Z Dictionary Online, s.v."Anus," accessed December, 2012http://www.dreammoods. com/dgibin/dreamdictionarysearch. pl?method=exact&header=dreamsymbol&search=an us.

Chapter 1

4. Proverbs 18:21 (Amplified Bible).

5. American Osteopathic College of Dermatology (Dermatologic Disease Database *Keloids and Hypertrophic Scars*; accessed 2005), http://www.aocd. org/skin/drmatologic_diseases/keloids_andhypert. html.

6. Melissa Conrad Stöppler, *Cysts,* ed. William C. Shiel Jr, accessed 2010, http://www.medicinenet. com/cysts/article.hhtm#tocb.

7. Pastor Henry Wright, *A More Excellent Way: 1 Corinthians 12:31 – A Teaching on the Spiritual Roots of Disease* (Georgia: Pleasant Valley Church, Inc., 2002).

8. Pastor Henry Wright, *A More Excellent Way: 1 Corinthians 12:32 – A Teaching on the Spiritual Roots of Disease* (Georgia: Pleasant Valley Church, Inc., 2002).

Chapter 2

   9. Steve Hein, *Emotional Intelligence,* accessed 2011, http://eqi. Org/ehon.htm. P. 36.

Chapter 4

   10. Dream Moods A-Z Dictionary Online, s. v."Ears," accessed December, 2012.

   11. Psalms 24:4 (The Way, The Living Bible Series).

Chapter 6

   12. "Birth Order and Personality" on Samantha Murphy's official website, accessed 2010, http://www.birthorderandpersonality.com/id15.html (site disconnected).

Chapter 8

   13. Psalms 139:14 (The Message).

Chapter 9

   14. The Talking Drum Online, s. v."The Willie Lynch Letter – Greetings," accessed 2005, http://www.thetalkingdrum.com/wil.htm.

   15. The Talking Drum Online, s. v."The Willie Lynch Letter – Greetings," accessed 2005, http://www.thetalkingdrum.com/wil.htm.

   16. Jesus Is Lord Online, s. v."Incubus & Succubi," accessed 2005, http://www.jesus-is-lord.com/incubus.htm.

Chapter 17

   17. Psalms 139:14 (King James Version).

Segue Way

   18. Minnie Riperton, *Memory Lane*, Lyrics. Time, A. LyricWeb. Site, all Minnie Riperton-Memory Lane lyrics, artist names and images are copyrighted to their respective owners, posted by The Cave, http://www.lyricstime.com/minnie-riperton-memory=lane=lyrics.html. Accessed 2012.

Concludes with a Few Additions
Stages of a Child

19. The *Child Development Institute Parenting Today Blog*; "Stages of Social-Emotional Development-Erik Erikson," blog entry by Child Development Institute Parenting Today, accessed 2011.

Soul Wounds

20. Dictionary Online, s. v."Soul," accessed 2011, http://www.dictionary.reference.com/browse/soul.

And Once Again

21. Steve Hein, *Emotional Honesty,* accessed 2011, http://eqi.org/ehon.htm.

Mention

1. *Harry Potter and the Sorcerer's Stone*, author, J. K. Rowling.
2. AMC's *Mad Men*.
3. Motown's, Martha Reeves and the Vandellas, "Dancin' in the Streets" 1964.
4. CBS's *The Jeffersons*, 1975-1985, "Movin' on Up," theme song co-written and sang by Ja'net Dubois and Oren Waters.
5. "Work That" from *Growing Pains* (a song by Mary J. Blige).
6. *Nancy Drew Mystery Stories – Series Books* by Carolyn Keene.
7. *Coffy*, written and directed by Jack Hill, 1973.
8. *Cleopatra Jones*, directed by Jack Starrett, 1973.
9. The Black Panther Party, originally known as the The Black Panther for Self-Defense, a revolutionary socialist organization active in the United States from 1966 until 1982.
10. Kool & the Gang, an R&B, funk, and jazz band, originated in the '60s.
11. Ohio Players, funk & R&B band that was extremely popular in the '70s.
12. *The Negro Speaks of Rivers*, poet Langston Hughes, 1921.
13. Angela Davis, American political activist, author and scholar. In the '60s, she was an activist with the Communist Party USA, affiliated with the Black Panther Party and Civil Rights Movement and has long been an advocate for prisoner's rights. She is the

founder of Critical Resistance an organization working to do away with the prison-industrial complex.

14. *Mandingo*, novel by Kyle Onstott, 1957.
15. *Falconhurst*, novel series by Kyle Onstott, 1964.
16. "The Infantry has Landed (and They've Fallen off the Roof)," an episode of *The Cosby Show*, NBC.
17. *Perry Mason*, a television series about a defense attorney based on a detective fiction authored by Erle Stanley Gardner that ran from September 1957 to May 1966.
18. *It's a Wonderful Life*, based on the short story "The Greatest Gift", written by Philip Van Doren Stern in 1939, and movie classic directed by Frank Capra, 1946.

Permissions Acknowledgements

Thank you so much for giving me permission to utilize your invaluable information:

- *A More Excellent Way: 1 Corinthians 12:32 – A Teaching on the Spiritual Roots of Disease:* Definitions of cysts and obesity by Pastor Henry W. Wright. Copyright © 2002 by Pleasant Valley Publications.
  BE IN HEALTH GLOBAL, 4178 Crest Highway, Thomaston, GA 30286. www. BeInHealth. com
- DreamMoods. com: Definition of "earlobe," and "anus." Dream Moods Media Division.
- Steve Hein, author, *Emotional Intelligence,* accessed 2011, http:/ /eqi. org/ehon. htm

Dirty Breath: Trapped by Rejection by Lana M. Hooks

For speaking engagements, virtual or brick and mortar book signings you may contact PharSide Coed Book Club at:
Pharsidecoedbc@gmail.com
Or
678.579.5930/404.437.1869

Subscribe and join the author for online discussions called "#authenticsoultalk" on her blog/vlog www.lanamhooks.com. It is here she will discuss how to dispel the dirty breaths. Also for purchasing her memoir and signing up at her website she will send you a free gift!!!

Lastly, she would love to hear from you about your 'dirty breaths,' because we are all on this road together. And please make sure you give her a review on CreateSpace and Amazon. We have to keep spreading the word about Emotional Abuse! Awareness is crucial to our wholeness and healing.

Thank you for taking your precious time to read her memoir. She hopes that it helped you remember your pictures, snapshots, and fragments on your journey to be emotionally authentic. Namaste.

—————————————————

www.ingramcontent.com/pod-product-compliance
Lightning Source LLC
Chambersburg PA
CBHW072122270326
41931CB00010B/1637